Peggy Matteson, PhD

Advocating for Self: Women's Decisions Concerning Contraception

Pre-publication
REVIEWS,
COMMENTARIES,
EVALUATIONS . . .

"**T**his is a concise, well-written, pragmatic, and important book for both health and mental health care professionals such as nurses, social workers, physicians, and others who deal with women's health-seeking decisions and behaviors. Focused on contraception decisions, the author, a nurse, lays out an extremely important five category model of women's decision-making, which she conceptualizes, overall, as 'Advocating for Self.' In this model, women make conscious, reality-based choices that place them in control of their own bodies, hence, their own futures, so that they have opportunities to take advantage of multiple and fulfilling educational and employment options.

As a researcher in the feminist tradition, the author uses women's own voices to vividly describe their reality. The author challenges existing assumptions about women's contraceptive behaviors, assumptions which themselves derive from faulty past theories about women's development and behavior. The importance of listening to women's own voices when trying to understand behavioral decisions is wise advice for all health professionals."

Nancy W. Veeder, PhD
Associate Professor,
Boston College Graduate School
of Social Work

"**D**r. Matteson's book reframes how women go about making decisions regarding the use of contraceptive methods. Based on qualitative inquiry, she has developed a substantive theory that takes into consideration the complex decision making that women undergo and how various facets of women's lives impact these decisions. Listening to the women's voices, which are ever present in the book, the reader comes to understand that fertility regulation is an ongoing process, and that women base their decisions on relational theory and life circumstances. When 'Advocating for Self,' women weigh their own life obligations as well as the views of others. Although they do not always successfully prevent pregnancy, they consider other ways in which choices can benefit them.

This book should be welcomed by health care providers who counsel and provide family planning services. It helps us understand that while each woman is unique, there are similarities in their decision making that providers can take into account when teaching women about options in contraceptives. In particular, the section on providing appropriate contraceptive care (Chapter 7) outlines a women-centered approach to working with women, and offers a model in which women become partners in their care, and one that is holistic in nature and helps women define for themselves which methods meet their personal criteria for use."

Linda C. Andrist, PhD
Assistant Professor,
Graduate Program in Nursing,
MGH Institute of Health Professions,
Boston, MA

More pre-publication
REVIEWS, COMMENTARIES, EVALUATIONS . . .

"*Advocating for Self: Women's Decisions Concerning Contraception* by Peggy Matteson opens new ways of thinking about why some women have trouble using their chosen methods effectively. Dr. Matteson notes correctly that health care providers tend to counsel clients about initiating contraceptive use but do little, if anything, to help them build problem identification and problem solving skills for continued use. Dr. Matteson's understanding of a feminist approach to health care leads her to see the importance of each woman's 'personally constructed knowledge' and her own lived experience. Effective use requires consistency with both her understanding and feelings about methods and her lifestyle.

For clinicians, Dr. Matteson points out that 'most women are not making their contraceptive decisions based on the rational, prescriptive perspective.' She also points out that partners can have a major influence on both the quality and continuation of method use. Rather than label women who have use problems as noncompliant, Dr. Matteson argues that clinical care must be redesigned to take a more holistic, continuous view of appropriate contraceptive care. The partner's role also needs to be taken into account in providing care.

This book should be helpful to clinicians who are striving to develop new approaches that can be more helpful to problem users, especially those who seek contraception and then return with an unintended pregnancy. The framework and qualitative case quotes will also be of interest to researchers who wish to build a better understanding of how contraceptives are actually used."

Deborah Oakley, PhD
Professor of Nursing,
Center for Nursing Research,
School of Nursing,
University of Michigan

Harrington Park Press
An Imprint of The Haworth Press, Inc.

Advocating for Self
Women's Decisions Concerning Contraception

HAWORTH Innovations in Feminist Studies
Esther Rothblum, PhD and Ellen Cole, PhD
Senior Co-Editors

Advocating for Self
Women's Decisions Concerning Contraception

Peggy Matteson, PhD

Harrington Park Press
An Imprint of The Haworth Press, Inc.
New York • London

Published by

Harrington Park Press, an imprint of The Haworth Press, Inc., 10 Alice Street, Binghamton, NY 13904-1580

Library of Congress Cataloging-in-Publication Data

Matteson, Peggy.
    Advocating for self : women's decisions concerning contraception / Peggy Matteson.
       p.   cm.
    Includes bibliographical references (p.   ) and index.
    ISBN 1-56023-868-2 (acid-free paper: pbk.).
    1. Contraception–Decision making. 2. Self-efficacy. 3. Contraception–Psychological aspects. I. Title.
RG136.M383 1995
613.9′4′019–dc20   95-14297
                                                        CIP

This book is dedicated to all of the women who have so freely shared their time and very personal life events with me in a joint effort to improve the quality of health care that women experience.

ABOUT THE AUTHOR

Peggy S. Matteson, PhD, is Assistant Professor in the College of Nursing at Northeastern University in Boston, Massachusetts, and a certified OB/GYN nurse practitioner. She has published, researched, and presented on topics related to nursing, maternal care, women's health, and women's choice and use of contraceptives. Dr. Matteson is a member of a variety of professional organizations and serves on the Executive Committees for the Council for Advanced Nursing Practice and the Council of Maternal Child Health of the American Nurses Association. She is also a media expert on women's health for that association and a consultant for J. B. Lippincott Company Division of Nursing Books.

CONTENTS

Foreword

When a woman chooses a method of contraception, the act of choosing is only one step in the decision-making process. Her choice of contraception, moreover, is not a life choice, but an event in the context of her life at one point in time. Each method has a failure rate, and method efficacy relies to a greater or lesser degree on a woman's decision to continue use over time. Most disconcerting to health care providers who attempt to assist women with the decision-making process are reports by women that they chose not to use a method, did not fill a prescription, or consigned the diaphragm to the drawer. Where, we ask ourselves, did the miscommunication occur during the choosing process?

Dr. Matteson's research helps us to understand the many factors women consider when they choose and use a method. Her work refutes claims that contracepting is a linear process or that women progress in choices from less to more effective methods. She explores how women integrate contraception into their lives and why they sometimes cannot do so, even when they do not desire a pregnancy. Her choice of a feminist framework implies empowerment for women in the decision-making process. And it challenges those readers who are health care providers to help women to empower themselves, rather than capitulate to a paternalistic model of care delivery.

How then can we do a better job when women come to us for help in the process of choosing? Are we asking the right questions to empower women to choose methods they really can integrate into their lives? Are we listening when women tell us about their difficulties integrating contraception into their lives?

This book is a guide for all health care providers who assist women with choosing contraception and for women who are considering contraception.

Joellen W. Hawkins,
RNC, PhD, Boston College

Preface

My particular interest in studying women's patterns of fertility regulation developed from interactions I had with college women when I was an obstetrical/gynecological nurse practitioner at their student health clinic. Repeatedly, women would make appointments for the purpose of initiating a contraceptive method. They would complete the appointment and leave, implying that their needs had been met and that they would be using their chosen method. A startling number of these women returned at a later date, either for a pregnancy test or for a post-abortion examination, because they had discontinued use of their selected method while remaining sexually active. Often they then restarted their method of choice or switched to a new method, only to return again in the near future. Later, discussions of this phenomenon with middle-aged women stimulated them to share with me their patterns of contraceptive usage over a broader time frame. They too reported various patterns of selection and discontinuation.

I began to wonder how other women who practice contraception managed their experiences of fertility regulation within the framework of the activities of their lives. A search of the literature provided some insights as to what causal factors other researchers had investigated. However, few studies had asked women their experiences or views concerning this process. The realization that I needed to ask women these questions in order to develop a greater understanding of the phenomenon in which I participated as a provider stimulated me to formulate the format, purpose, and questions of the study that has resulted in this book.

Acknowledgments

This book could never have been written without the assistance and support of many people.

First, I am grateful to the women who gave of their time and privacy to share their fertility regulating histories with me. Their thoughtfulness, candor, and endorsement of this work will always be remembered.

A special thanks to a very supportive mentor, Dr. Joellen Hawkins, who helped an idea take root, grow, and finally flower into this finished product. Our stimulating discussions, as well as her continued support and encouragement, inspired me to be creative, extend myself, and believe in my convictions.

In addition, thanks to Susan Burr, Ellen Christian, Pat Gardiner, Kathy Hodgkins, and Karen Wheeler, who stimulated and nurtured the initiation of this project.

A very special thank you to Bill, Jenny, Eric, and Ryan, who are always there showing an interest, encouraging me, and providing me with the space and time in which to work.

Chapter 1

The Impact of Fertility Regulation in a Woman's Life

For centuries, heterosexually active women have been held hostage by the risk of pregnancy. No single health care development has provided the means to directly alter women's lives as momentously as the development of contraceptive methods. The use of relatively safe, effective contraceptive methods provides a means to end the history of death, chronic illness, fatigue, and unfulfilled potential which has been imposed on women by unintended pregnancy.

Each time a woman becomes pregnant, her body responds to support the developing fetus. Pregnancy, while beneficial to the survival of the species, creates a risk of increased morbidity and mortality for the individual women. With the experience of multiple pregnancies, a woman's physical health may be affected, her aging process hastened, or death may occur during the gestational or delivery process. Numerous pregnancies and unspaced births not only affect a woman's health, but reduce her economic productivity and increase her dependency on others for support during pregnancy, childbirth, and/or childrearing periods.

Fertility regulation is a conscious choice with which a sexually active, heterosexual woman can positively affect her physical, educational, economic, and social destiny. When a woman uses a highly effective method of contraception, the principal outcome is the reduction in the incidence of unplanned pregnancy. Able to control her fertility, she gains the opportunity to plan her life as she limits family size or prevents pregnancy from ever occurring.

An ability to control the occurrence of pregnancy influences not only her personal health and economic well-being, but also her ability for intimate interactions with significant others.

Knowing she is capable of controlling her childbearing abilities also broadens a woman's vistas in the development of a broad variety of life opportunities. Able to prevent or defer childbearing, a woman may pursue educational opportunities and participate in various ways within the labor force. Contraceptive use enables a woman to select when a pregnancy might occur. Planned births can be integrated into a working woman's career more readily than unplanned births, therefore, the potential for a negative impact on her employment situation or career development may be reduced.

Some women are successfully demonstrating the multiple options education and employment offer them when effective contraception is possible. Other women have not been as adept in their attempts. Instead, they have learned by experience that few things limit a woman's life as much as the fear of conception or the reality of an unintended pregnancy.

Why is it some women are experiencing success while others' efforts are being thwarted? What are women's experiences with using contraception? Is there a universal process which all women go through as they consider contraceptive use? What are the obstacles to successful contraceptive use? What facilitates success? Can we learn factors from successful women which may help others also achieve fertility control?

Health providers currently hold varied opinions concerning women's contraceptive beliefs and practices. Appropriate care can be provided only if these beliefs are reality based. To learn about women's actual experiences we must listen to their voices, unobstructed by prior assumptions. In order to develop a practice which supports the reality of women's contraceptive beliefs and practices, it must be based on women's lived experiences.

CONTRACEPTIVE USE IN THE UNITED STATES

Fertility surveys conducted in the United States provide evidence that many women attempt to use a variety of contraceptive methods to control their reproductive lives. In 1988, the most recent national estimates of contraceptive use indicated 90 percent of the women currently at risk for unintended pregnancy were using contraception. Sterilization, either female or male, was the leading method of choice with 23.6 percent of contracepting couples choosing this permanent method. The use of oral contraception was selected by 18.5 percent of those interviewed, while the use of male condoms was the choice of 8.8 percent. The diaphragm, periodic abstinence, withdrawal, the intrauterine device (IUD), and all other methods available at the time were chosen by 9.3 percent of the respondents (Mosher and Pratt, 1990).

Surprisingly, when contraceptive method efficacy rates are compared, women who practice contraception experience unintended pregnancy at a higher rate than expected. That is because effectiveness in preventing an unintended pregnancy is dependent not just on the protection offered by the method itself, but on how consistently and correctly it is used. Due to these variables, the probability of becoming pregnant while practicing contraception is considerably higher than the published efficacy rates which are calculated on conditions of perfect use. In addition to the theoretical or inherent limitations of a contraceptive method, deficiencies in the way it is used contribute to actual failure rates (Jones and Forrest, 1989).

Assumptions about women and their seemingly ineffective contraceptive practices are prevalent in both the popular and professional literature. Expectations concerning women's behaviors have resulted in the development of health care practice protocols based on myths, inferences, and the male perspective of women's life experiences. Therefore, they are not reflective of the limitations and problems women experience.

Insights developed from women's actual experiences indicate that previously held assumptions may no longer be true. Forty women, with a combined total of 310 contraceptive years, agreed to share their experiences surrounding contraception. They are a diverse group ethnically, educationally, and economically. During their attempts at contraception they have been single, married, and for some, single again. Some have used contraception in an attempt to totally prevent unintended pregnancy while others have used it for child spacing. These women's stories reflect a broad range of lived experiences illustrating their varied contraceptive beliefs and practices. The differences in their experiences are interesting, the similarities are enlightening!

PAST ASSUMPTIONS AND BELIEFS

The following are some of the assumptions which continue to be applied to the health care of women long after being published by Gerrard, McCann, and Geis (1984). Each is an inaccurate premise of care, as the reality of women's lives reveal very different perspectives.

Women Are Ignorant About Contraceptive Methods

Many presume that unintended pregnancies occur when women fail to take precautions because they are ignorant about the contraceptive options available to them. However, many women can list from two to 13 different methods to prevent pregnancy. They garner their information from a variety of sources such as health classes, books, magazines, reports in the media, friends, and/or family members. A woman's age is not a factor in the scope of her knowledge.

Women Are Unaccepting of Their Sexuality

Women not only acknowledge their sexuality, but act in response to sexual desires as they seek relationships which become intimate. An interest in contraceptive methods demonstrates acceptance of possible sexual activity and that pregnancy may result from these behaviors. Seeking professional assistance to cope with this risk indicates they not only acknowledge their sexual activity to themselves, but are willing to acknowledge it to others.

Women Lack Access to Care

Women find ways to access care from various sources. They are resourceful and network with other women. Even young adolescents learn how they may acquire the contraceptive health care they desire. However, knowledge of sources does not always lead to the accessing of care.

Women Have Irrational Fears About Specific Contraceptives

Women express fears about certain contraceptive methods. The most common concerns are about oral contraceptives. The fears are based on the potential side effects providers warn them about, reports in the media about the possible increased risk of breast cancer, and the negative experiences of friends. Concerns surrounding the use of an intrauterine device (IUD) are the result of media reports, the withdrawal from the market of some devices, and reports from friends who have used IUDs. Fears about bodily changes after tubal ligations are based on reports of difficulties from friends who have experienced the surgery and from occasional warnings surfacing in the media.

To label these fears as irrational demonstrates a provider bias. Each woman bases her concerns on some form of evidence. After the historical experience of using women as guinea pigs in contraceptive research, the degree of skepticism which some women express about the safety of certain methods may in fact be an indication of rational behavior (Boston Women's Health Book Collective, 1992; Dreifus, 1978; Frankfort, 1972; Seaman and Seaman, 1977). In the absence of evidence that a woman's fears are blatantly irrational, the benefit of doubt about the effects of a method belongs to the woman.

Women Are in Conflict About Birth Control Use

The conflict women express is not whether they should practice contraception. The conflict exists over which method provides the best protection and yet interferes the least with their lives. Creating a viable balancing act becomes the focus of women's actions. They wish to adopt a contraceptive method which will provide protection from pregnancy without disrupting their sexual experience or the many other facets of their lives.

Women Do Not Understand that Unprotected Intercourse May Lead to Pregnancy

Women are aware of the link between unprotected intercourse and the potential for conception, otherwise they would not seek ways in which to protect themselves. In fact, understanding this relationship and hearing repeated warnings about the risk of unprotected intercourse even leads some women to assume they are unable to become pregnant. When a pregnancy does not occur after an episode of unprotected intercourse, they start to believe that they might be infertile and unable to become pregnant. Use of contraceptive methods is therefore not enhanced by teaching this process as a simple cause and effect relationship. In order to develop a more accurate knowledge base, women need to learn more about their fertile periods and understand why unprotected intercourse does not always lead to conception.

PAST THEORISTS' EXPLANATIONS OF PATTERNS
OF CONTRACEPTIVE USE

Other researchers have attempted to explain women's patterns of contraceptive use. In 1972, Lindemann, using grounded theory, developed a theory of contraceptive method sequencing which involved a three-stage pattern of birth control choices. She proposed that women upgraded their practice of contraception in stages from nonuse, to use of nonexpert methods, to use of a method supplied by an expert.

Eighteen years later, the majority of women do not display this progression from nonuse, to peer methods, to expert methods (Matteson and Hawkins, 1993). Today more than 55 percent of women report the use of some form of contraception with their first incident of intercourse. The initial method chosen by 42.9 percent of these women is the pill, diaphragm, or intrauterine device, all methods which Lindemann classifies as expert methods. The remainder follow Lindemann's described sequencing by using peer prescription methods: condoms (51.43 percent), foam (2.86 percent), or withdrawal (2.86 percent) as their first contraceptive methods.

In 1976, Miller, reporting on interview data collected prior to 1971, proposed what he termed as "a natural sequencing of contraceptive behavior" among women, as they changed from one method to the next. He reported they begin with the use of abstinence itself, or periodic abstinence such as rhythm or withdrawal; progress to the coitus-dependent methods: foam and/or condoms; and then move to prescription methods: oral contraceptves or the diaphragm. He stated that when trying to assess an individual's sexual and contraceptive behavior, the present location of a woman within this proposed developmental sequence needed to be identified so that her future contraceptive behavior could be anticipated. He also suggested that once a woman interacted with a health care provider concerning contraceptive methods, she would select and then remain with a prescriptive method.

Twenty years later, women do not report following this developmental plan either. The majority do not progress from an abstinence method, to a coitus dependent method, to a prescription method. Only 2.86 percent of modern women report using withdrawal as the initial method. The remainder start with a coitus dependent method (54.29 percent) or a prescription method (42.9 percent). Therefore, the knowledge of what method a woman is currently using is not, as Miller suggested in 1976, an accurate predictor of her next method choice. Some women's actual patterns of use indicate that they start with the use of a prescription method and later return to a coitus dependent method or an abstinence method.

Miller also suggests that interactions with health care providers increase a woman's contraceptive vigilance and the use of prescription methods (Miller, 1976). Current data make it apparent that some women, even when receiving annual gynecological examinations from a health care provider, change permanently from the use of a prescription method to a nonprescription method.

CURRENT CONTRACEPTIVE DECISIONS

The contraceptive practices described by women today do not follow the models of either Lindemann (1972) or Miller (1976). Women now appear to be choosing contraception in a manner different from what was attributed to women 20 years ago. No new theories have been developed, yet previous assumptions no longer explain women's current contraceptive practices.

To fill the current gap in information concerning the phenomenon of female contraceptive use, ascertaining women's own descriptions of their experiences and concerns becomes critically important. Of particular importance is the development of new insights and theories based on women's lived experiences. Scholars have become increasingly aware that a woman's orientation to her relationships is a central component of the female identity and emotional activity. Without consideration of the experiences of the relational, connected female when considering contraceptive behaviors, the true richness of women's experiences are being ignored.

The rate of unintended pregnancies occurring in today's women who practice contraception reflects the complexity of factors a woman must address and the underlying difficulties between a user and her method. If a woman is serious about preventing a pregnancy, she might be expected to choose a method with the highest efficacy of prevention. However, women who seek the care of a health care provider do not always choose and continuously use the more efficacious prescription methods. Women change from one method to another in various patterns of selection, some increasing and some decreasing the efficacy of their protection from pregnancy. For previously unexplained reasons, some women, even after receiving the assistance of a health care provider, are unable to choose and then consistently use a reliable method.

What could explain this seemingly erratic behavior when a woman says she does not want to become pregnant? Based on stories and explanations offered by the women themselves, a substantive theory entitled Advocating for Self has developed. Women's experiences indicate that they are making decisions about contraceptive practices while attempting to successfully integrate the process within the complexity of the rest of their lives. As women explain, the primary factor influencing the ability to consistently use a method is the ability to integrate the chosen regimen of use without disrupting the patterns of their daily lives.

ADVOCATING FOR SELF

In a woman's world, no facet of life stands alone. This is especially true when considering a relational process such as sexual intercourse. Each woman is in an interactional relationship with at least one other person when forced to deal with fertility regulation. When a woman participates in heterosexual activity, she is faced with the realization that these endeavors may cause her to become pregnant.

For a sexually active woman who is at risk for pregnancy, controlling her fertility becomes a recurrent decisional process. Advocating for Self describes the fertility regulating process as experienced and described by modern women. It is comprised of five decision categories which are sequential in nature, have a degree of overlap between them, and create a circular process which continues as long as a woman is at risk for pregnancy. While Advocating for Self in using contraceptives, a woman acknowledges that preventing pregnancy is only part of her life, and therefore the process may only be effectively dealt with in a manner which attempts to keep it in balance with all other aspects of life.

In order to understand this decisional process, each of the phases must be understood in relationship to the others. When a woman chooses to control her fertility, she enters a decision-making process comprised of sequential steps. Some women progress through the steps rapidly, choosing and staying with a specific fertility regulating option for many years. Others move more slowly through the steps of the cycle or return repeatedly to the beginning of the cycle. Surprisingly, even the use of a method for a long period of time does not mean that the woman's evaluation of the contraceptive risk and action of the method has ceased. Whether changing methods or not, women continue to evaluate their method choices related to other factors in their lives. (See Figure 1.1.)

Personalizing Pregnancy Risk

The initial stage, Personalizing Pregnancy Risk, may occur in a new or continuing heterosexual relationship when the potential for sexual intercourse exists. It reflects a woman's essential

FIGURE 1.1. Advocating for Self: A Theoretical Model of a Woman's Process of Fertility Regulation

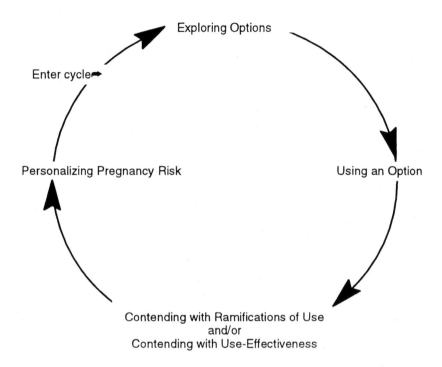

awareness of her ability to become pregnant and the understanding that if she chooses, she has the ability to prevent this from happening. When at risk for unintended pregnancy most women choose to attempt in some manner to minimize the occurrence of the experience.

Exploring Options

The decision to explore options is a personal one, subject to many outside influences. The second step, Exploring Options, is comprised of an evaluation by the woman of her perceived contraceptive options and the effect the use of each would have on her life. A woman explores options already known to her or suggested by friends, a family member, or a care provider. The option with the least negative consequences, as the woman envisions it, will be the one she selects to use. When she is more uncomfortable with the thought of using any method, the option to continue to be at risk for pregnancy is still available to her.

Using an Option

The use of a contraceptive method does not automatically follow the selection of one. These two actions are based on separate decisions. The third step, Using an Option, includes the use of any intervention which a woman believes will reduce her chances of becoming pregnant. The decision to use a method (IUD and Norplant) remains subject to active reevaluation by some women with each event of use. So, even after a method is chosen and available, some women do not use it in a way which would provide the highest degree of protection. These women explain that erratic use results from ambivalence concerning use and from the desire for as pleasurable a sexual experience as possible.

Most women assume the responsibility for contraception within a relationship, especially when a female method is chosen. When the occasion of need actually presents itself each woman again explores her feelings regarding its use. She decides if her desire for fertility control is being met in a manner which does not detract from the sexual act and if it is appropriate to her overall needs.

Once a woman uses a method, she enters the fourth step of the cycle. She must deal with the ramifications of use including side effects, the level of peace of mind she obtains from her method, or an actual pregnancy if one occurs. These considerations determine a woman's future contraceptive course of action.

Contending with the Ramifications of Use

After a contraceptive option has been exercised, a woman determines how she feels not only about the mechanics of use, but also about her experience with the contraceptive action itself. This step, Contending with the Ramifications of Use, occurs when a woman identifies the consequences of these specific actions and evaluates the tradeoffs for herself. As a woman weighs the efficacy of a method against the actual ramifications she experiences, she decides whether to use it again, decrease the frequency use, stop use, or return to a personal evaluation of her risk for pregnancy and start the decisional cycle again. This is a common phenomenon, as women average between two and three method changes while coping with the fertile years of their lives.

One of the results of being sexually active is having to deal with a monthly concern about the prospect of an unintended pregnancy. When a woman's menstrual cycle is late in occurring, the concern about pregnancy is handled in different ways by various women. Some seek support, especially from their friends. Others seek information about how to determine if they are pregnant and what options are available to them.

No matter what method a woman uses or how conscientious she is about its use, each woman maintains a degree of awareness that she could become pregnant. The degree of concern varies, independent of the method she is using. Women on the pill, a method with a high efficacy rate, express as much concern as women using withdrawal, a method with a low efficacy rate.

If the onset of her menses remains delayed or an actual pregnancy is diagnosed, this reinforces a woman's personalization of the risk of pregnancy. The concern about or actual occurrence of a pregnancy sends a woman back to the step of Personalizing the Risk. She then begins again to Explore Options. The result of this may be that she remains with her original contraceptive option, chooses a new option, chooses to risk pregnancy with unprotected intercourse, or eliminates her risk by abstaining from sexual intercourse.

A more in-depth exploration of each of these steps will provide an opportunity for the women to speak for themselves. Their life experiences were different, yet the themes they dealt with were universal across the group. To understand women's needs concerning contraceptive activity requires an exploration with them of the particularities of the individual experiences.

SUMMARY

Women who are sexually active in heterosexual relationships are at risk for developing a pregnancy unless they or their partners take steps to decrease the odds of it occurring. Studies conducted in the United States indicate that most women attempt to prevent pregnancy from occurring for at least part of their fertile years. Unfortunately, even when women are using contraceptives, pregnancies occur at a higher rate than expected. There are many past assumptions and theories about why this occurs. However, these do not concur with the process which modern women describe. Drawing on explanations offered by women themselves, a substantive theory entitled Advocating for Self provides new understanding of the decisional process women pass through and the factors which impact on their decisions concerning the use of contraception. This model explains a process that is cyclical in design, has four steps, and is entered when a woman recognizes she is at risk for pregnancy.

REFERENCES

Boston Women's Health Book Collective (1992). *The new our bodies, ourselves.* New York: Simon and Schuster, Inc.

Dreifus, C. (Ed.) (1978). *Seizing our bodies–The politics of women's health.* New York: Random House.

Frankfort, E. (1972). *Vaginal politics*. New York: Quadrangle Books, Inc.

Gerrard, M., McCann, L., and Geis, B. (1984). "The antecedents and prevention of unwanted pregnancy." In A. Rickle, M. Gerrard, and I. Iscoe (Eds.), *Social and psychological problems of women: Prevention and crises intervention* (pp. 85-101). New York: Hemisphere Publishing Co.

Jones, E. F. and Forrest, J. D. (1989). "Contraceptive failure in the United States: Revised estimates from the 1982 National Survey of Family Growth." *Family Planning Perspectives* 21(3), pp. 103-109.

Lindemann, C. (1972). *Birth control and unmarried women*. New York: Springer Publishing.

Matteson, P. and Hawkins, J. (1993). "What family planning methods women use and why they change them." *Health Care for Women International,* 14(6), pp. 539-548.

Miller, W. B. (1976). "Sexual and contraceptive behavior in young unmarried women." *Primary Care,* 3(3), pp. 427-453.

Mosher, W. and Pratt, W. (1990). "Contraceptive use in the United States, 1973-1988." *Advance Data from Vital and Health Statistics of the National Center for Health Statistics.* (Number 182, March 20). Washington, DC: U.S. Department of Health and Human Services.

Seaman, B. and Seaman, G. (1977). *Women and the crises in sex hormones*. New York: Rawson Associates Publishers, Inc.

Chapter 2

Personalizing Pregnancy Risk

In the model of Advocating for Self, personalizing pregnancy risk occurs when a sexually active woman becomes aware that not only is she at risk for pregnancy, but also that she has the opportunity to affect the outcome of her sexual activities. Some women are able to make a realistic connection with the abstract realization that heterosexual intercourse presents a risk of pregnancy. Others must have a personal experience in order to have this potential become real for them. Feelings of uncertainty about the reality of pregnancy risk and the actual protection provided by contraception permeates this phase. Each woman explores her potential risk either by using a protective measure before intercourse initially occurs, or through her response to the amount of fear generated by an act of unprotected intercourse.

AWARENESS OF PREGNANCY RISK

A woman may learn from many sources that if she has sexual intercourse, she can become pregnant. However, this remains a hypothetical concern because acknowledging that intercourse could lead to pregnancy, and personalizing that it can actually happen to her, are two different concepts.

As Cindy and Esther reflected on how they each became pregnant at age 16, they revealed they had knowledge but were out of touch with reality. Even though they had both been taught about the risk of pregnancy, each remembered being surprised it actually happened after participating in unprotected intercourse. Cindy said, "We had only done it (intercourse) a few times so we were surprised." Esther's thoughts were, "[I] didn't think I would get pregnant because we weren't doing it often enough." For each of these women, a pregnancy resulted from the knowledge deficit that even a limited number of incidents of unprotected intercourse can result in pregnancy.

Other women expressed a lack of internalization of the risk by maintaining the belief that "it can't happen to me." This lack of personalization of a risk resulted in delays in considering protective action. Frances related that when she was 16 years old, "[getting pregnant from intercourse] was the farthest thing from my mind." When Gerri was 19, she had an experience of unprotected intercourse and then quickly adopted the use of male condoms. Gerri said she used condoms for six months and then started using the pill. She related that she used contraception "[because I was] paranoid about getting pregnant but I didn't really think it would happen to me." Helen also expressed similar sentiments: "[At age 15, I] didn't think [I] could get pregnant. I had a sense it can never happen to me."

The previous three women were reflecting on the thoughts they had had as adolescents. Yet being older did not automatically determine that a woman had internalized the actual risk she was taking with unprotected intercourse. Ivy, currently age 31, said, "[I] wouldn't panic about the possibility of pregnancy until after sex was over." However, Ivy continued, "[I] really didn't think it would happen to me."

For some women, it took an actual experience with pregnancy for the concept of pregnancy risk to become personalized. Jane, at age 17, found herself pregnant after having unprotected intercourse. She revealed, "It feels different now that I got pregnant. I guess I was too young [to really understand the risk of pregnancy to me]."

Acting on the encouragement to use contraception, women feel that by taking action they are making themselves safe from the risk of pregnancy. However, the reality that the risk of pregnancy continues even while using contraceptives, is a difficult concept for some women to maintain. Kaitlyn, a 34-year-old interior designer, had experienced five pregnancies while continuously using one of six different contraceptive methods. She explained, "I was surprised that I became pregnant because I thought I was taking care of it [by using contraception]."

DEALING WITH DOUBT

After women internalize their potential for pregnancy, motivation to explore ways to protect themselves decreases when pregnancy does not occur after an act of unprotected intercourse. Louise explained, "Since I didn't get pregnant the first time [I had unprotected intercourse] I thought I couldn't get pregnant. That made me feel relieved, and yet it also scared me that maybe I could never get pregnant. The possibility of pregnancy continued to haunt me. I was happiest when sex wasn't planned and we wouldn't have them [condoms] to use."

Louise was torn between the fear that she could not get pregnant and a desire to see if she could even though she did not want to have a baby at this time. This conflict of desires did not stop her from using condoms. However, it did lead her to take chances with unprotected intercourse when condoms were not available. Being carried away by the mood of the moment put her at risk for pregnancy, and she could test the reality of her fear of infertility. Each time she experienced unprotected intercourse and still did not get pregnant, her worries grew that she might never be able to get pregnant.

When a woman assumes she is infertile or at least that it would be difficult for her to conceive, she may become less vigilant. This was the case of Mary, who at age 17, used the pill for contraception. She stopped when her relationship ended, fearful that "using it could permanently affect me and make me sterile. I had heard a lot of scary stories about the effects of the pill. I felt like a guinea pig. I thought that using it might prevent me from getting pregnant in the future." When a new relationship began, she was less concerned about contraception because her fears about infertility had escalated: "I thought the pill had destroyed me and that I was barren." Over the next two years, Mary used a partial abstinence method she developed for herself. Calling it the "grace method," she described it as just not having intercourse when she thought she was ovulating. The end result of using this method was that a pregnancy occurred. Mary speculated that maybe her timing of abstinence was off because "I had a secret passion to get pregnant." After her child was born and placed for adoption, Mary then returned to the use of the pill.

AWARENESS OF PREVENTIVE OPTIONS

Most women possess an awareness of contraceptive options from which to choose which will, if not eliminate, at least decrease their chances of becoming pregnant. They learn about these from friends, classes, books, advertisements, health care providers and/or family members. However, the awareness that such options exist does not automatically lead to selection and use. Each woman's experience differs, in perceiving her pregnancy risk and then acting in a preventive manner. Intervening factors impact to individualize the process of integrating contraceptive tools into each woman's sexual practices.

INFLUENCES OF PARTNERS

During most of their reproductive years, women spend much of their time avoiding pregnancy. Reasons given for not wanting to become pregnant are: it would interfere with the continuation of education; it would create financial insecurity; a medical condition would pose a health risk to the fetus; or a pregnancy would create problems within the couple's relationship.

Nancy, currently age 24 and working in bank operations, started being sexually active nine years ago. Since becoming pregnant at age 19 while using her contraceptive method choice of withdrawal, she has alternated periods of abstinence with short periods of oral contraceptive use. Six months ago, fearful that a pregnancy would interfere with the relationship she was developing with her current boyfriend, she chose to use the pill as her method choice. She explained, "There is no way I want to screw up this relationship by getting pregnant."

When a partner is older than a sexually inexperienced woman, she may allow him to assume the initiative for contraception. Except when they have strong religious beliefs, men do not generally object to the idea of their partner using female contraceptive methods. When objections do occur, they are generally toward specific methods for very individualized reasons.

Some partners encouraged the women to consider going on the pill. Others asked women to stop the pill because of the mood changes experienced by the users. Nancy shared her experience: "the pill made me grumpy and moody. Like (I) had bad PMS all the time. I was just bitchy . . . and I resented Wally because I had to go on the pill." For Nancy, the outcomes of use caused her and her partner to choose to discontinue use of the pill. Instead they chose to use withdrawal, which later resulted in an undesired pregnancy.

Some partners are of little assistance in helping women adapt to the reality of a potential pregnancy. Some are unaware of when a woman is at risk for pregnancy. Others just do not give the preventive process the same priority women do.

Most women try to discuss with their partners the potential for pregnancy and their desire to prevent it. These conventional attempts sometimes result in assistance in the contraceptive process. Men may come to view contraception as a shared responsibility and agree to assist in the process. The degree of assistance they offer ranges from agreeing to use a condom to actually sharing in the purchase of supplies, such as a diaphragm and contraceptive jelly or oral contraceptives. Since the expense of oral contraceptives may run as high as $25 a month, sharing expenses in this manner helps more women maintain the use of this method.

However, some women have found even when a partner indicates he desires to prevent pregnancy, this may not necessarily be true. This was most evident from the scenario which Ora, age 24 and unmarried, related. She and her partner had agreed to use male condoms to prevent pregnancy. She liked this method because "he had to worry about it." Once they had initiated condom use, she did not give it a further thought and the incidents of intercourse continued over many months. Then she realized their relationship appeared to be gradually changing, and this made her uncomfortable. She recounted that two weeks after an episode of intercourse he called and "out of the blue asked if I had gotten my period. When I told him yes, he hung up. I have not heard from him again." Attempts on her part to contact him were futile. She suspected that, in an effort to trap her into a more permanent relationship, during their last episode of intercourse he did not use a condom, hoping she would become pregnant.

Married women and their husbands often adopt a less vigilant stance than single couples. The reasons for this change are expressed as the desire for more enjoyment of the sex act and the desire for child spacing rather than pregnancy prevention. For Beth, the enjoyment of sex within marriage was sometimes more important than contraception: "We decided to stop trying to prevent pregnancy since it [putting on the condom] wasn't any fun."

Esther explained that she and her husband experienced a real sense of ambivalence: "We sort of wanted another child then, even though we thought financially we should wait." After Esther experienced strong physical reactions to the pill, she and her husband resumed the use of condoms. "We've never had one break, but if we did we would welcome the child. I enjoy being pregnant. It's just that I'm getting older [age 35] and that worries me. My scoliosis makes me uncomfortable when I'm pregnant, so I wouldn't choose it. But if a pregnancy happened, we would welcome the child as a gift."

Both of these couples express an awareness that unprotected intercourse can lead to an unplanned pregnancy. They did not have an active desire for a child. What they did desire was pleasurable intercourse and relief from the side effects of oral contraception. To meet these goals, the couples chose to have unprotected intercourse or moved to a less efficacious method, removing the responsibility for the choice of a child from their actions. They did not actively seek another child, they just ended the activity of vigilant prevention. With this action, the careful weighing of advantages and disadvantages of another pregnancy and a definite decision to proceed toward pregnancy never had to occur.

INFLUENCES OF OTHERS

An important consideration for many women was their perceptions of the positive or negative attitudes of family or friends toward the women's decisions to practice contraception. Beyond that, Roman Catholics also mentioned the tenets of their religion as a constraint to considering the use of contraception. Other women, especially adolescents, explained a delay in considering the idea of contraception because they could not bring themselves to talk to their mothers about it. Some women believed their parents would "kill them" if they knew they were even considering the use of contraception. Gerri, a 20-year-old receptionist, hid the fact that she was using oral contraception by carrying her pill pack with her at all times. She felt there was less chance her mother would find them in her pocketbook than in her room.

Penny, a 25-year-old bank teller, explained: "My parents would freak if they ever knew. They are real old. My dad is 80. I have older sisters, but no one has ever talked about any of this. I have to hide the pills and everything from them. I need to keep it [indicates the bag with the condoms, vaginal film, and pills] locked in the glove compartment of my car."

Rather than having to hide the fact they were considering contraception, other women were actually encouraged by family members. This type of encouragement may be a factor that has developed in more recent times, as only women in the younger half of the sample mentioned such supportive behavior. Some women reported that they sought care or were actually brought to a care provider by a close family member. A majority of the time it was their mothers. Rose was 18 and had been sexually active for four years when she was taken to a birth control clinic by her mother. At age 15, Rose had been using condoms for protection and had beome pregnant. After the termination, she used the diaphragm with condoms and developed bladder infections. Concerned about her daughter's contraceptive history and her future, Rose's mother insisted she go on the pill.

When they were 16, Sandy and Trish were brought to a clinic by their mothers, to receive contraceptives before they became sexually active. Anticipating the actions and desires of their daughters, each mother wanted her daughter protected before pregnancy could occur.

When she was 17, Wendy had sex for the first time and used condoms for protection. After trying several types and colors, she talked to her mother because she did not like the way condoms felt. "I told my Mom about the experience and she brought me to a [private] doctor to go on the pill."

Sisters (with or without the knowledge of other family members) and peers are also helpful in pointing out the risk of pregnancy and in suggesting sources for information and methods. Some accompany the woman when she goes in for care. Ann cited her sister as being the most helpful influence to her in choosing and then effectively using a contraceptive method. Ann was 17 when she and her partner chose the condom for protection. However, they did not like the way it felt and Ann remained fearful about becoming pregnant. For help she turned to her sister. "She talked to me [about contraception], she set up my appointment and she came with me." The support and assistance of her sister resulted in Ann becoming an effective user of oral contraceptives.

CHANGES IN RELATIONSHIPS

Some women were unable to make the connection between the risk of pregnancy and the need for contraception until they viewed themselves in a serious relationship. For some, the awareness of the need to practice contraception developed as the seriousness of the relationship increased. Women became more consistent in a method's use or switched to a more efficacious method as the relationship intensified and the partner became a "steady boyfriend" or a "fiancé." This phenomenon of greater diligence also occured at a point when the frequency of intercourse increased from once or twice a month to once or twice a week. Motivation toward more effective contraception appeared to come from a change in how a woman viewed herself within the intensifying relationship.

When Mary became sexually active at age 15, she "saw sex as a sport" and something done "for status." During this time she viewed the use of contraception as tedious and described it as such. "Foam was messy, tedious, too wet and it decreased sensations. I don't like 'messy' when I have sex so we often didn't use it. The diaphragm was tedious getting it ready, putting it in just before and then caring for it afterwards. I would skip it 25 percent of the time rather than go through the whole routine." Her attitude did not change until age 17 when she settled into a relationship with one partner and then sought care so she could use the pill. When that relationship ended, she went off the pill and used abstinence during ovulation with subsequent short-term partners. As the seriousness of her current relationship developed, she chose to use condoms and then returned to taking the pill.

Barbara, age 25, a full-time waitress and part-time student, related a similar scenario although she did not become sexually active until the age of 19. After first using condoms, Barbara switched to foam and condoms and then experimented with the contraceptive sponge. After two years, she and her boyfriend had developed a "steady relationship and we wanted to get married," so she sought professional assistance and went on the pill. Differences between the couple developed, she explained, then "we broke up and I didn't date for a year. I went off the pill because I couldn't see spending money when I had no prospects and I didn't want casual sex." When she started dating again, she abstained from intercourse for two years and then progressed back to using condoms. It was again two years into her current relationship before she sought professional assistance and resumed the use of oral contraception.

SUMMARY

A woman's awareness of her personalized risk of pregnancy develops in an individualized manner. This is the process which occurs in Personalizing Pregnancy Risk (refer to Table 2.1), the first step of the Advocating for Self decisional model. Once aware she is truly at risk for pregnancy, a woman may or may not seek information about possible options. It remains an individualized decision, heavily influenced by a woman's view of herself, by other's actions, and by the woman's perceptions of others'

TABLE 2.1. Personalizing Pregnancy Risk

Causal Condition	Phenomenon	Context	Intervening Conditions	Actions/Interactions	Consequences
potential for sexual intercourse	**Personalizing pregnancy risk** –awareness of the ability to become pregnant and that options exist	awareness of pregnancy risk: minimal– acute	woman's age	gathers more information	decides whether contraceptive action is worth the risk
properties: –new or continuing heterosexual relationship		awareness of options: minimal– extensive	partner's age, motivation	examines feasibility	
			woman's perceived beliefs of her mother's attitude towards contraception	weighs possible consequences to self, others	
			experiences of friends/sisters		
			frequency of intercourse		
			seriousness of relationship		

27

views of her sexual activity. Some women discuss the ideas of contraception with their partners, sisters, or mothers. Others assume it as a personal responsibility which they maintain even as their partners change. Some women successfully insist their partners assume at least part of the responsibility for obtaining contraceptive supplies.

Women evaluate the feasibility of initiating pregnancy prevention by considering the possible consequences it will have on their self-esteem and physical health, as well as on their relationships with family and current partners. Based on these considerations, their choices vary, from deciding to do nothing while proceeding as before, to talking with others and exploring contraceptive ideas further as they continue experiencing unprotected intercourse, or to deciding to abstain from intercourse until a method is chosen and available.

Chapter 3

Exploring Options

After determining that her sexual activity places her at risk for an undesired pregnancy, a woman must explore what contraceptive options are available and acceptable to her. The number of methods she knows about and her knowledge about how to obtain them limits the scope of these considerations. Most of the women in this study knew of at least one method of contraception which could be used during the first experience of intercourse.

Ann, age 17 at the time, selected condoms for her first experience with intercourse because "it was the only thing I knew about at the time." Her boyfriend made the use of condoms a viable option within their relationship after he agreed to purchase and use them.

Two other teenage women provided examples of variations in how women act on their knowledge about contraception. "I didn't know much about anything except condoms and they aren't accurate," Connie said. Because of her concerns about becoming pregnant while using condoms, she explored what other options a 15 year old might have. After finding a clinic and learning a government program would pay for oral contraception, she chose to start the pill. Ruth also selected the pill for contraception before starting intercourse. She explained that when she chose contraception, "I select[ed] by the percentage of protection and by my comfort with putting the drug in my body." In other words, she chose her method based on efficacy rates and on fears she had about what its use could do to her body.

Women select a particular contraceptive method for a variety of reasons. Over the course of a span of time, the reasons for selecting a particular method of contraception might change, but the method itself will stay the same. Conversely, the woman's reasons for selecting a specific method might stay the same, but the method used will change as a woman tries to find one which actually meets her desires.

CONVENIENCE IN OBTAINING A METHOD

In order for a woman to consider a method as a true option, she must be able to obtain it. Convenience in obtaining a method is important to women and is sometimes the only reason a certain contraceptive method is selected for use. The methods women find most convenient to obtain are foam, the sponge, and the male condom.

Convenience led Mary, at age 15, to choose foam as her initial method for two reasons. She "could be anonymous" when she obtained it because she did not have to disclose herself to someone she knew and because of its "easy availability." Mary explained, "I could just walk into any drugstore and buy it for myself."

Other women stated they selected condoms for the same ease in availability. Condoms became the preferred option for Rose and Louise because the use of them did not entail making a visit to a health care provider. They each expressed a positive view of condoms, but for slightly different reasons. Condoms were selected by Rose, at age 15, because they involved "the least procedure, no doctor was needed so I didn't need an appointment or anything." However, due to the embarrassment of disclosing her planned sexual activity at the checkout, she only bought them occasionally. The majority of the time she relied on her boyfriend to supply them.

Fear, not ease, led Louise, at age 17, to choose condoms. She "was scared of going to a doctor. I was afraid [that after an examination he would tell me that I didn't need them,] that I couldn't have children." However, she made her partner responsible for buying the condoms. Also when 17 years old, Paula selected condoms because "they were the easiest for my age group to get." She had considered using oral contraception but "the pill scared me with all of the things it can do to your body."

Becky and Liz both explained their choice of condoms was due to the fact that their only alternative was to have unprotected intercourse. Limited access to other options led Becky, at age 15, to insist her boyfriend supply the condoms for them to use. She said, "[It was my] only access to anything and I didn't want to do it with nothing."

Lack of anticipatory planning led Liz, age 16, to select condoms as her method because it was the only contraceptive means obtainable when she needed it: "It was the only thing I had access to, to prevent pregnancy." The risk of pregnancy even with the use of condoms concerned her, but the ease of accessing condoms from machines and stores led her to choose that option again and again.

EXPENSE

Almost all contraceptive methods cost something to initially obtain and then use on a continuing basis. Even the accurate use of the Basal Body Temperature method requires the purchase of a specific thermometer.

The potential financial drain of oral contraception was a concern voiced by many women. Elaine was 17 when she first chose the pill as her contraceptive method. Even though she was comfortable with her choice, she said, "[the] money to pay for the pill is a concern and [it created] a hesitation [in my selecting it for use]." She went on to explain that the continuing expense was one of the reasons she would discontinue use when her relationships broke up. Even when she expected to quickly meet another man and develop a new intimate relationship, she could not justify the continued expense of using it until that event occurred.

Melissa, age 26, considered oral contraception her best method choice as she definitely did not want to become pregnant. However, she described the cost of the pill as "a real problem" and a potential deterrent for serious use.

Unless the cost is covered by a health plan, women often mentioned the cost of contraceptive supplies as a deterrent to choosing any one of them for continuous use. Yet it is interesting that none of them compared the financial cost of using a contraceptive method against the cost of an abortion or the cost of raising a baby.

CONVENIENCE OF USING A METHOD

The pill and the intrauterine device (IUD) are the only two methods which women mentioned as convenient to use (Norplant was not yet readily available). Many women explained they decided to change from using condoms to using the pill because "it is convenient and easy to use."

Gerri started using condoms at age 19. However, the aggravation of having to stop to put it on was one of the reasons she discontinued that option and considered using oral contraception. Unable to pay the full cost of the prescription herself, she was only able to consider it a viable option when her boyfriend offered to pay half of the cost.

Like Gerri, convenience also led Ora to move from using condoms to selecting the pill. Ora said, "[I] knew a lot of people on them and I knew I'd be protected against pregnancy. [It] seems like the easiest [method] because it's always in the system." She was helped in the implementation of her option because the cost was covered by her health insurance.

Laurie, at age 19, started using the pill as her first contraceptive choice. She opted to start with the pill because "there was nothing to worry about" and it "wouldn't interfere with intercourse."

Expressing similar desires of not wanting "to have to think about it" led Ivy and Sharon to select very different choices. Ivy, at age 22, moved from opting for the diaphragm to selecting the pill. The fact that she was able to obtain the pills for free made it possible for her to act on this desire and she successfully continued to use oral contraception for the next six years. Similar thoughts led to a different choice by Sharon, as she moved from using the pill to having an IUD inserted at the age of 17. She chose the IUD because her insurance would pay for it (and not the pill), and since she had difficulty swallowing tablets, she would not have to worry about ingesting a pill every day.

EFFICACY

The degree to which a method would prevent a pregnancy from occurring was a primary consideration for some women and was the reason they often gave for selecting the pill. For Laurie, who initiated the use of the pill at age 19 before she started having intercourse, this method offered "the surety of not getting pregnant." Even though she remained consistently concerned about having to remember to take the pill and experienced the side effects of weight gain and complexion problems, the desire for high efficacy caused her to remain on the pill until her intimate relationship ended.

The need for extreme caution led Melissa, a 26-year-old graduate student, to ignore all other methods and make the pill her first and only contraceptive choice. She chose the pill because she "thought it was the most effective and most convenient method." However, this decision was not without reservations: "I don't like taking medications generally and I wonder, is it healthy? I do like the fact that it evens out my temperament, [so there are] no more bad mood swings and my [menstrual] cramps and blood flow have decreased. Friends tell me it [taking the pill] is not healthy [so I'm concerned. However, I] can't risk pregnancy due to my family circumstances. They wouldn't accept a lack of virginity. My father is a Southern Baptist minister, my brother is a missionary, my sister is in seminary. I attended seminary and went on a mission trip." Melissa's desire for the method with the highest efficacy led her to reject the consideration of any other methods, and to opt for a method which causes her some concern but statistically provides the best protection against pregnancy.

Donna switched from using condoms to using the pill at age 21. Because it was easy, she used the pill for about three years, eventually discontinuing use when she stopped having intercourse. At age 25, after returning to using the pill, she experienced an increase in weight and more prominent premenstrual symptoms. For symptom management, her pill was changed and in the process she became pregnant. After resolution of the pregnancy, she resumed contraception with the diaphragm as her choice. She explained she "didn't like the side effects of the pill" and now knew she "could get pregnant on it." Therefore, she no longer considered it a viable contraceptive option. The experience of side effects was not bearable when the level of pregnancy protection was not absolute.

After delivering a son from an unintended pregnancy, Carol, at age 22, chose the pill because "I wanted to use something to prevent another pregnancy. It was the safest in that I wouldn't get pregnant again right away." Unfortunately, Carol found the pill "made me feel weird, crazy in the head." She explained, that she "tried different types but none of them agreed with me." Fearful of having "something in me" with the IUD and afraid that a diaphragm might become stuck, she opted to use condoms be-

cause they were the "next best thing to the pill for protection ...
from disease as well as pregnancy."

The degree of efficacy of a certain method was also the reason
some women rejected a method. Fear of pregnancy caused
Becky to ultimately reject the option of withdrawal. When she
was 16, Becky and her partner had switched from using condoms
to using withdrawal. They felt it was "more natural." Becky also
felt it "was making him responsible," as she "had trust that he'd
do it." The biggest drawback for her was a constant "worry that
it wouldn't work" and she would become pregnant. This led her
to "hope that if it happened, the guy would be a gentleman" and
help her with the pregnancy. After living with this uncertainty for
two years, Becky returned to using condoms. She explained it
was the "only access [she had] to anything" and she "didn't
want to [continue to] do it with nothing."

SAFETY

The safety afforded by a contraceptive method is an issue for
women which expresses itself in one of two concerns: protection
from sexually transmitted diseases, and physical safety for the
woman.

Protection from Sexually Transmitted Diseases

Very few women express an active consideration of protection
against sexually transmitted diseases, including human immuno-
suppressant virus (HIV), when exploring contraceptive methods.
Their reasons are that they care for their partners, believe the
feeling is reciprocated and cannot imagine their partners being
infected. Since they cannot see signs of infection, their partners
must be "clean." Several exceptions to this type of thinking
occurred after women had contracted a sexually transmitted disease (STD) from a partner. Again it seemed that experience
became the best teacher to motivate realistic action.

After using the pill, then the sponge, then the pill again, Laurie, at age 26, considered condoms as a top priority option. After having experienced genital warts, she "[did not] want to catch anything else." Even though neither she nor her partner "like the feel of condoms" and it affected their "spontaneity," using them made her "feel safer from STDs." In the future she expects to add another contraceptive method to this process to increase efficacy. However, she knows her options are reduced as she does not like the effect oral contraceptives have on her body, she has no interest in the diaphragm, and an IUD is "scary to have in [the] body."

Jane chose oral contraception as her first method. When the relationship broke up, she stopped using the pill. When a new relationship developed, she selected male condoms because of their "pregnancy and disease prevention" qualities. After experiencing an unintended pregnancy, she has reviewed her options and combined the use of condoms and the pill. Her reason for choosing this action was that "rubbers protect [me] against both pregnancy and disease."

Physical Safety

Women examine their method options and then eliminate certain methods because of concerns about their personal safety from use of them. The variety of effects some women experience when using the pill creates the most concern. When this level of anxiety occurs, most choose the barrier methods of diaphragms or condoms instead.

In 1979, at the age of 16, Mary chose the "diaphragm because I wasn't brave enough for the pill. [I] felt like I was a guinea pig. . . . I thought that using it could permanently affect me and make me sterile. [I thought it could] prevent my getting pregnant in the future."

Similarly, Ivy, at age 18, chose the diaphragm as her first method option because she "didn't want to go on the pill. It was too big of a jump to go from nothing to the pill. [I] didn't have a boyfriend but I wanted it for protection when necessary." For Eileen, a 19-year-old college student, using the diaphragm "seemed logical . . . because I didn't want the pill. . . . [I] don't like taking medications at all. . . . [The diaphragm] seemed safe and it was comfortable."

Concerns about her physical safety also led Paula, at age 17, to choose the condoms as her initial method option. The "pill is scary with all the things it can do to your body."

The option of the diaphragm is also rejected by some women. The idea of having to touch themselves in the vaginal area to put it in prevented Ann, a 21-year-old hairdresser, Penny, a 25-year-old bank teller, and Ruth, a 24-year-old graduate student, from considering the diaphragm as a method choice. The idea of having a foreign object in their bodies stopped both Elyse and Nancy from considering the diaphragm as an option. Elyse explained, "I don't like the idea of putting it in even though I'm in touch with my body." Also, not completely sure it was worth the effort, she continued, "[I have] heard about diaphragm babies." Having used four different contraceptive methods and experienced two unintended pregnancies, Nancy still would not consider the diaphragm as an option. She would not want to put it in because she has a "hard enough time with a tampon."

Other concerns were also expressed by women. Fearful that she "would insert it wrong" caused Louise to reject the diaphragm as an option. Carol rejected it because she thought the diaphragm might get stuck inside.

Many women share concerns about using the IUD. Few women have heard positive comments about it. Some have concerns about having it put in and the increased chance of an infection developing. The idea of a foreign object, plastic or metal, remaining in them was labeled as "scary" by many. Sandy, at age 26, had difficulty considering it as a viable option because she was concerned it could perforate her uterus, or fall out and not protect her from pregnancy. Accounts of problems, either their own or of friends, led most women to reject the IUD as an option. Specific family experiences concerned two women and prevented each of them from considering it as a choice. Maryann refused to consider the IUD because her "Mom had trouble with it." Liz had the same negative attitudes because her aunt became permanently infertile after having one inserted. Several women stated that because of their fears, they would reconsider it as an option for personal use only after they had all the children they desired.

The overwhelming reason given for not choosing a method as a contraceptive option was the fear of personal harm. The women's decisions as to what methods were options for them were based on other women's experiences which were either told to them personally, related by a friend, or reported by the media. Oral contraception and the IUD led the list of methods rejected as options because of fear of personal harm.

INFLUENCES OF PARTNERS

Male condoms are the only true contraceptive method which men are capable of implementing as a method choice option. Having heard about condoms from her friends, Linda, at age 18, thought "it seemed like the easiest way. My partner got them so it was less embarrassing." Barbara, when she was 19, reported that her partner "chose the condoms." She said she allowed this because "he was a lot older than me and experienced."

Some partners are not supportive of condom use. They refuse, complain about, or delay in using the condom. In general, women reported that men hate condoms. As Melissa said, "Men hate condoms. Whenever I broach the subject of using them each has said, 'Well, we might as well break up.' "

Being unprepared for intercourse leads a woman to be dependent upon her partner in making such a method choice. When

Frances, at age 16, found herself about to have intercourse, she "wanted to be cautious about pregnancy and disease. I asked him if he had them [condoms] and he did so we used them." Later there were "no condoms available so we used withdrawal." In both instances she depended on his choice and cooperation. She later remedied this by choosing the pill.

INFLUENCES OF OTHERS

Friends, relatives, and health care providers all influence the contraceptive options a woman perceives she has. Their efforts either provide full support, support her choice within selected methods, or they make the decision and impose a selected method upon her.

Friends

The experiences of friends have an impact on the options a woman might even consider. Linda, a 20-year-old usher, would not consider the diaphragm because "I'm not adventuresome. A couple of my friends have used it [diaphragm] and gotten rid of it." Having heard from others that "jelly makes such a mess," Sharon, a 23-year-old hospital unit coordinator, also rejected the diaphragm as an option.

The experiences of other women can also have the positive effect of leading a woman to investigate an option she might not have otherwise tried. Ivy, age 31, had already used and disliked the diaphragm, pill, and condoms, and felt uncomfortable with using the IUD. She did not know what option to choose next. She just knew she "didn't want the pill or an IUD." A friend's recommendation of the cervical cap led her to seek more information and a source for that option.

Familiar with the fact that friends used the pill led Ora, at 24, to stop using condoms and consider the pill as an option. She explained, "I know a lot of people on them. I know I'll be protected against pregnancy."

Relatives

Sisters are also helpful in broadening a woman's consideration of various contraceptive methods, by suggesting methods or advising her how and where to obtain them.

A woman's relationship with her mother may have either a negative or a positive impact on the spectrum of her choices. Becky, at age 16, had been sexually active and using condoms for a year and a half when she chose to change to the use of withdrawal for protection. She knew about the pill but was not comfortable in selecting it as an option. Becky explained, "I didn't choose the pill because I couldn't talk to my mom about it."

In contrast, Maryann, at age 18, was able to talk to her mother, which resulted in having a positive influence. Maryann explored using either the diaphragm or oral contraception and chose the diaphragm as her first option. Maryann explained that the choice was influenced by her mother: "She said it was the most effective and I was hesitant to take the hormones of the pill."

Her mother's example also led Sandy, a 34-year-old lawyer, to choose the diaphragm as her contraceptive option when she was 26 and after already having used oral contraception, an IUD, condoms, and the sponge. Sandy explained that she finally reached this decision because, "My mother had used it and it worked for her."

Health Care Providers

Care providers also affect the type of options that a woman perceives she has. Kaitlyn, an interior designer, reported that at age 33 she decided to obtain a diaphragm. She "went to be fitted for a diaphragm and the doctor said to use the sponge. That it was just as good." For that reason, she changed her method of choice to the sponge.

Doctors' recommendations led Jane and Wendy, both age 17, to consider the pill as their best option. When Sharon, at age 16, went to seek contraceptive care she found herself with no other contraceptive alternative except the pill as that "was all that the clinic offered." However, since she had always been unable to swallow any type of tablets, this eventually proved not to be a viable choice for her. Carol, age 28, had three children and wanted pregnancy protection through a tubal ligation. However, her physician refused to consider this option, saying that she was too young.

Some women are limited in their contraceptive options because they will not seek the services of a health care provider. Reasons given for this are: fear of a gynecological exam, reluctance to have a male physician examine them, or fear that their family might find out they are sexually active. Describing her parents as very strict, Liz chose to use condoms for protection because her parents would not know. When she went to her family doctor for a routine checkup at age 17, her doctor asked her if she was sexually active. Only after the female doctor reassured her that she would not tell her parents, Liz admitted that she was having intercourse. The doctor then provided her with the pill as a contraceptive option.

By the age of 22, Nancy had experienced several painful interactions with physicians, resulting in damage to her self-esteem. To determine which methods were options for her, she evaluated her apprehensions concerning doctors and gynecological procedures and weighed them against her fear of pregnancy from using a less effective method. She selected withdrawal and then condoms as her first method options. She remained with these until an unintended pregnancy brought her back into gynecological care and provided the pill as an option. However, when her prescription ran out she went back to using condoms rather than make a return visit to the gynecologist. It was not until a friend referred her to a clinic staffed by female nurse practitioners that she would again consider a prescription method of contraception as a viable option.

SUMMARY

Individual factors affect women's options for contraceptive protection. (Refer to Table 3.1.) It became apparent after hearing the women's stories that what generally occurred in the selection of a contraceptive option was first, the elimination of methods for various reasons, and then, the remaining method(s) became the only true option(s).

No woman views the entire spectrum of contraceptive methods as a collection from which she can freely choose. Some limit their range of options because even though they can obtain a method, they have concerns about its effect on them. They would then eliminate that option from further consideration. In actuality, women demonstrate that an option often is not chosen because it is the most desirable, but because it has the least negative consequences.

When a woman is concerned about the side effects of each of the options she believes are available to her, she determines that there is no true contraceptive option for her. The physical risk of incurring a pregnancy as compared to the risk of attempting contraception is not a consideration that is verbalized.

After each woman evaluates her contraceptive options, a course of action occurs. She chooses and possibly uses a method, or she continues the task of exploration by collecting more information while postponing a choice, or, distraught or overwhelmed by the idea of using contraceptives, she stops her consideration of all possible contraceptive options.

TABLE 3.1. Exploring Options

Causal Condition	Phenomenon	Context	Intervening Conditions	Actions/Interactions	Consequences
decision to investigate contraception	**Exploring options** –a personal evaluation of options based on conceptions of potential ramifications of use	knowledge of sources: limited-extensive	method's availability	considers efficacy, cost, side effects, convenience,	selects a course of action: either choosing or not choosing an option
properties: –personal decision –subject to outside influences		availability: easy-difficult	partner preferences and/or conditions of use	determines feasibility of using options	
		confidentiality: low-high comfort with	knowledge of mother's and/or friend's methods	eliminates options based on concerns	
		method source: low-high	view of health care providers		
			physical concerns		

Chapter 4

Using an Option

Selecting a method for contraception and actually using it are two very separate activities. Even after women find sources of information and care, make and keep appointments, pay for services and obtain a method, the actual rate of implementation and consistency of use of a selected method varies across women and across the type of contraception chosen. If the risk of pregnancy or the desire to prevent pregnancy decreases, or if the relationship changes, it could be more easily understood as to why a woman does not follow through with the implementation of her choice. However, if the risk of pregnancy and the desire to prevent it from occurring remain stable, the actual implementation and then consistent use of a method should routinely occur. In fact this does not happen. Some women obtain a method and then never use it. Others try a method once or twice and then stop. For others, using a method for even six months becomes an extended period of time. Patterns of consistent use are based on one or more of the following factors.

ATTITUDES TOWARD CONTRACEPTIVE USE

The attitudes that the women had toward to the act of using contraceptives were generally positive and supported the idea that contraception is necessary to maintain control of one's future. As Liz stated, "You have to, if you're not ready to have a baby. Even though it goes against my religion, I want a child when I can care for it." As much as fertility control is desired, some women acknowledged that for them, using contraceptives is not an effortless endeavor. "If it works it's fine. It's a lot of work but [it's] worth the effort," reported Ruth. Most of the women commented that they had not found it difficult to use at least one contraceptive method effectively. Yet, as Louise stated, "It's more difficult than not using it but I feel it is a necessity." She went on to explain that by using contraceptive methods, she felt she had gained a measure of control in her life which she has not had before.

FERTILITY CONTROL

Most women indicated that they viewed contraceptive methods as a form of self-protection, and each sought a method which could provide them with that type of control. Some illustrations of the value of this control were elicited by the question: "Do you feel you have control over your fertility?"

Becky had previously depended on condoms and had then used withdrawal. At age 18, she has chosen "natural family planning" (rhythm) because "with rhythm I was in charge. I knew when I was safe from pregnancy." Frances, who also had a history of using condoms or withdrawal, explained that using these methods made her feel insecure since her partner controlled the process and there was more of a chance of her getting pregnant. She explained that she began taking the pill because "I trust myself more than anyone."

Helen used condoms when she started having intercourse at the age of 15. At age 18, she has changed to oral contraception, and expressed similar reasoning: "[I feel that] with the pill, I have control. It's my responsibility. I [now] understand it well. It's an everyday thing and I don't have to run to the store at the last minute."

For Melissa, age 26, using oral contraception was against her strong religious convictions, and she initially avoided it as a possible choice. However, she reported that by age 22 she had "decided that I wanted to stop fighting off the men I was dating. I was not sure I wanted to start [having] sex but I wanted to stop being [a] policeman. I felt it could make future decisions about sex more mutual." She specifically chose the pill, and has now used it for four years, because she "thought it was the most effective and the most convenient method." It also placed her in a position where the decision to have intercourse "would be about whether to have sex, not whether to risk pregnancy."

RESPONSIBLE USE OF CONTRACEPTIVE CHOICES

If the contraceptive methods chosen were the types actually used by women, most took responsibility for seeking out and obtaining the methods, and then implementing them appropriately. The female methods chosen for contraception were the pill, diaphragm, foam, sponge, rhythm, IUD, and suppositories. Using any one of these methods effectively requires some forethought and planning on the part of the woman.

Oral Contraception

Two women explained the routines they had developed to ensure they always took their oral contraceptives. Melissa strategized to develop a routine for herself to encourage consistent use by carefully selecting where to store her pill pack. Her solution was "putting my pills with my makeup. It helps me remember to take them."

Also concerned with consistency, Barbara thought of a way which would help her to remember to take her pill at the same time every day. "I took it when I pulled into the parking lot at work. You can never be late for work so I was never late with my pill." Using this structure put her at risk for inconsistency only on the weekend and work holidays.

Many women expressed pleasure with the freedom which the pill provided from preparing for each act of intercourse. However, their acceptance of the use of this method did not indicate freedom from concerns about the possible long-term effects on their bodies.

Liking "the ease of the pill" and "being responsible for self," Elyse still expressed concerns about an "increase in breast size" which was physically uncomfortable and "a fear of cancer developing." Although wanting the "responsibility of my own protection," Frances, and others who chose the pill, also worried about long-term use. For smokers this concern became even greater.

Many of the women using oral contraceptives also expressed concerns about future fertility problems. No one shared any scientific or anecdotal data on which they based their concerns, yet many repeatedly described the uneasiness they felt each time they exercised this option of taking a pill.

Condoms

If condoms were chosen, the male partner generally supplied them. Some women reported embarrassment purchasing condoms. As Louise related, "My partner had to provide them. I could buy them for friends as a joke but not for me as serious [business]. I was too embarrassed. [I] thought the clerk would know they were for me."

In certain relationships it became a shared mission. Ivy explained, "I drove him to the store and he bought them." Yet in other relationships, sometimes the man would agree to use them but the women had to supply them. When women found it difficult to purchase them, they sought out other sources such as friends and free samples from clinics.

For Rose, selecting and using condoms as a first contraceptive method, (at age 15) "was the thing to do. It made me feel like I was being responsible. [It was] satisfying because I wasn't getting pregnant."

Diaphragm

At age 26, Donna selected the diaphragm because she felt that it demonstrated "you are responsible for your own self." She reported that for the last 13 years she has used it 100 percent of the time when having intercourse and expected to continue in this manner.

After using condoms, the diaphragm, the pill, the diaphragm again, and then the sponge, Rose, age 23, has returned to the diaphragm. She explained that this became her final choice because she felt "safer, more secure. It felt like I was taking more personal responsibility."

Natural Family Planning

Women repeatedly explained that selecting and using a method option was not without its concessions. Selecting rhythm as her method so she "could be in charge," Becky found she still was not free from a "fear of pregnancy."

ROLES OF PARTNERS

The partners provided assistance to the women with verbal encouragement, supply of a method, and/or various other supportive actions. The women reported that when their partners were older or more experienced than they were, the men often tried to influence which method would be used. The chosen method might then involve the male controlled methods of withdrawal or the condom. Other times male partners pressured women into going on the pill. This option relieved the men from contraception responsibility and enabled couples to have more spontaneity in proceeding to the act of intercourse.

Supportive Actions

Several partners did help with the expense of the pill, either by reimbursing the cost or by alternating in purchasing the prescriptions. One man split the cost of the diaphragm and spermicide with the woman. Other partners found different mechanisms through which to take partial responsibility or assist in the contraceptive process.

Rose stated that when she started on the pill (at age 18), her "partner was real supportive and reminded me to take it." He also split the cost of the prescription with her. When the relationship ended two years later, she lost the emotional and financial support for its use and stopped taking the pill.

Sandy was 16 when she went on the pill, and then used it for three years. During that time she missed taking it only one or two times. She was responsible for obtaining it but her partner, who had encouraged her to use the pill, reminded her daily "so I didn't forget to take it." After switching to an IUD, condoms, and then the sponge, the diaphragm became Sandy's method of choice at age 34. Her partner helped her to be consistent in its use by reminding her to insert it: "He calls it the 'American Express Card' because I don't leave home without it."

When some women, such as Gerri and Becky, used condoms, they felt that their partners were supportive of their use; they did not make negative comments, they would buy them, and they were willing to stop to put them on. When condoms were unavailable, Becky and her partner chose to use withdrawal as their method. Sometimes these "condomless" incidents were casually planned because she felt it was "more natural" to experience intercourse without them. She had "trust that he'd do it [withdraw in time]" and "felt it was making him responsible" for contraception.

Because she chose to use an IUD, Sharon received a different form of support from her partner. She included him in the contraceptive process by having him "check for the string" to make sure the IUD was still in place and that she was protected against pregnancy.

Nonsupportive Actions

Penny's partner informed her that the use of condoms "bothered him." Therefore, he would agree to use them only occasionally. Based on similar experiences, Barbara agreed that "men don't like condoms." She explained, "My partner had a fit one night because I asked him to wear one. He apologized the next day but he still resists." Concurring, Melissa stated, "Men hate condoms. Whenever I broach the subject each has said, 'Well we might as well break up.'"

When men were resistant to using a particular method, the women often responded with acquiescence. When Sharon used the pill and forgot to take one, she tried to increase her level of protection against pregnancy by using spermicidal suppositories. Her partner resisted because he hated them, saying they were "disgusting, smelly, and create a runny discharge." Sharon found his response had a negative effect on her protective behaviors because "his dislike made me say 'oh well' and I wouldn't use them."

When a partner objected to a method a woman had selected, her method options became increasingly limited. This occurred for Eileen, who did not like "dealing with a diaphragm," preferring the ease of condoms. Her partner disliked condoms so Eileen tried using the cervical cap. After using the cap for several years she became pregnant. She stated that she felt "very frustrated, as my choices for further change seem limited. I don't feel comfortable with any other options." Eileen rejected using oral contraception because she did not like taking any kinds of medication. The IUD was not an option for her because she thought the idea of it sounded terrible and she was concerned about the physical problems it might cause within her uterus. Her partner's reluctance to use condoms continued to place her at risk for pregnancy, even if she did use the cap. It was not until she entered a new relationship, in which her partner was comfortable with the concurrent use of a condom and the cervical cap, that Eileen stopped worrying about getting pregnant.

REACTIONS TO USE OF VARIOUS METHODS

In addition to the supportive or nonsupportive actions of their partners, women had a variety of other reactions toward using specific contraceptive methods. These reactions depended upon a variety of factors.

Spermicidal Methods

Spermicidal foam, suppositories, and the sponge all created a general complaint: the discharge which follows use. One woman reported that the discharge was so heavy she had to wear a pad for the next 24 hours. Other women minimized this effect and expressed positive reactions to using these methods. It was not because they did not have the experience but because of the ease of use. For example, Kaitlyn found that during the three months she selected suppositories for use, they were "convenient, easy to get, and dead easy to use."

When Laurie found herself in a new relationship without time to restart the pill, she chose to use the sponge. She enjoyed the "convenience of putting it [the sponge] in only when needed and the spontaneity [it provided for an experience of intercourse]."

At age 18, Wendy chose to use the sponge for one month while waiting to start oral contraception. She found the sponge was convenient and not as messy as the use of the diaphragm had been for her. Two years later she chose to use foam and condoms while waiting for access to a provider in order to restart the use of oral contraception. She disliked these concurrent methods because of their impact on her sexual practices. She related that using these two methods decreased sexual spontaneity, made oral sex disgusting, and often meant the couple would not orgasm together as her partner would pull out after his orgasm "for better protection."

Barrier Methods

Methods which require the touching of intimate body parts, such as the cervical cap or diaphragm, caused discomfort for some women.

Cervical Cap and Diaphragm

When a freshman in college, Ivy did not have a boyfriend but she wanted to have protection. She anticipated that her desires for sexual exploration might make it become necessary. A visit to University Health Services provided her with the option of using the pill or the diaphragm. She explained, "I didn't want to go on the pill. It was too big of a jump to go from nothing to the pill." So she chose the diaphragm and used it for four years. However, getting used to inserting the diaphragm was not easy. Ivy explained, "I was young, unfamiliar with sex and embarrassed by the whole thing. It was like folding up a frisbee to get it in."

In contrast, Mary and Eileen expressed only enjoyment in using these barrier methods. Mary who began using the diaphragm at age 16, stated that, "once it was in it didn't bother me. It was easy to put in and I could share insertion with my partner." At age 21, Eileen appreciated using the cervical cap because "I can keep it in longer so it's more convenient. I don't have to put more spermicide in [with each act]."

Several women reported similar incidents which led them to stop using the cap. Complaining that short fingers made the process difficult, some described in great detail the process they went through to remove the cervical cap. One woman finally went to the hospital emergency room to have it removed because she just could not reach it. Obviously an incident such as this decreases a woman's desire to continue with the method.

Condoms

The male barrier method, condoms, also brought mixed responses from the women. Laurie's positive response was representative of many women, in which condom use was viewed as an enhancer of health and safety. Laurie reported she liked using them because "primarily I feel safer from STDs and secondarily I feel safer about pregnancy." However, she did not like how the method affected spontaneity, how it felt, or the hassle her partner gave her about using them. Yet these difficulties did not affect her implementation of its use. She just refused to have intercourse unless her partner complied.

Some women disliked the use of condoms and expressed two primary reasons. Mentioned most often was that the women had more enjoyable sexual sensations without using them. This change in sensation was reported regardless of the type or ribbing of the condom. The second concern was that the women disliked the disruption which occurred during the application of the condom. Very few of them took an active part in this process, as it had not been incorporated into the foreplay activity.

Ann spoke about the comparison between using and not using condoms: "[It] didn't feel natural compared to the first time when we didn't use it. . . . using it seems to be too much of a hassle, because we're disrupted. Several times it [the disruption] has almost led us not to use it." These concerns were echoed by Becky, who also experienced a reluctance to use condoms based on the difference in sensations. She explained, "Once it broke I knew what it felt like without it on." Her desire for a repeat of these sensations caused her to subsequently use condoms only 50 percent of the time, even though she continued to not want to be pregnant.

Intrauterine Device

Because of the health warnings provided by the media, most women would not consider having an IUD inserted. However, some of them had used it in the past. Kaitlyn, at age 19, had an IUD in for two months, until "it fell out." During that time, she enjoyed the experience because she "didn't have to think about it [birth control]." However, she remembered it was painful when it was put in and it created heavy bleeding during her menses, so she chose not to have it replaced.

Sandy was 26 when she had an IUD put in. She remembers that at first she "worried about perforation of the uterus, then figured since it hadn't happened I was okay." Sandy enjoyed it as a contraceptive method because she "didn't have to mess [with anything], it was painless and [I] didn't have to worry." At the end of the year she had it replaced with another IUD. After a few months this one was expelled. Sandy chose not to have it replaced again. Her reason was that memories of the insertion process generated memories of previous therapeutic abortions. Instead she chose to use a diaphragm.

Oral Contraception

Only two of the women in this group had never selected oral contraception as a method of choice for at least some short period of time. Most had used it for at least a few months, others had been happy with it as a method for years. In discussing why they had chosen to use oral contraception, most women cited the overwhelming advantage of its ease of use.

After first trying foam and then the diaphragm, Mary, at age 17, then selected the pill because "it was convenient, it regulated my cycle, and my periods were not as heavy or painful." Rose started using condoms at age 15, then used the diaphragm. At age 18, she selected the pill because "these are no contraptions to fiddle with."

These feelings were echoed by Elyse: "It was easy, convenient, and we could be spontaneous. We can do it [intercourse] anywhere with no worry. Because I was 15 I didn't like the idea of a diaphragm. Taking the pill was easier. I take vitamins every day and take the pill with them."

When oral contraception was an acceptable method choice, the problems most commonly reported by women were difficulties in continuing to be able to afford it and to remembering to take it daily. Sharon experienced a unique combination of difficulties when she attempted to use oral contraceptives. Sharon explained that at the age of 16, she went to a birth control clinic for assistance. The only method they offered her was oral contraception. She attempted to use the pill for 18 months and found that she had difficulties remembering to take it. However, when she did remember, she encountered another barrier: she had difficulty swallowing it and would gag. Further inquiry revealed that Sharon had difficulty swallowing tablets of any type. Under these circumstances, she found it difficult to maintain the use of the pill.

SUMMARY

Selection and then implementation of a contraceptive option are two different actions. Actually using a contraceptive method involves a separate decision, one which takes place each time an action is needed to implement contraceptive use. (Refer to Table 4.1.) The constant opportunity for reconsidering the decision to use contraceptive protection (except with the IUD) allows the woman the opportunity for a wide variation in actual utilization. The realistic implementation of a contraceptive method is determined by a woman's attitudes regarding its use, her perception of personal fertility control and responsibility, the supportive or

TABLE 4.1. Using an Option

Causal Condition	Phenomenon	Context	Intervening Conditions	Actions/ Interactions	Consequences
potential for sexual intercourse	**Using an option** —the use of an intervention that is believed will reduce the chances of becoming pregnant	option available: freely–with constraints	attitudes regarding use	uses option	evaluates this contraceptive action
properties: desires to prevent pregnancy		use comfort level: low–high	desire for fertility control		
		level of conviction: low–high	desire for contraceptive responsibility		
			roles of partners, peers, family, health care provider(s)		
			individual response to option		

57

nonsupportive behaviors of her partner, and the woman's response to the actual use of her selected method. For as long as
she chooses to use contraceptives, each woman retains the opportunity to reevaluate her course of action after each episode of
implementation, and possibly make a choice not to contracept
the next time. Few women choose to seek out the assistance of a
health care provider when they encounter difficulties with the
utilization of either prescription or nonprescription methods.
They do not view them as collaborative partners in their contraceptive activities.

Chapter 5

Contending with the Ramifications of Contraception

No method of fertility regulation is guaranteed to be absolutely successful. Along with the lack of absolute assurance, each option also presents the potential for negative ramifications. Using a method during intercourse or in anticipation of intercourse may not be a problem for some women. But having to deal with the effects of a method during or after intercourse may lead to some situations which make women uncomfortable. Women explained that contraceptive use may have physical, emotional, sexual, or health and safety ramifications. No method was exempt from having some women find that it had a distasteful sequel of use.

PHYSICAL RAMIFICATIONS

Physical ramifications are classified by women as having from minimal to severe effects. These effects may be constantly present, occur only as the method is used, or occur only subsequent to the act of intercourse. Some women find the side effects are severe, and that they interfere with their activities of daily living, such as relating to others and caring for children, or disrupt their sense of physical well-being.

Distasteful Sequels of Use

Using contraception led to sequels of use which some women found distasteful. Women spoke about experiencing discharges, odors, and bleeding. Some disliked using spermicides and termed them "messy." Ruth found the discharge after using spermicidal suppositories was "so gross" that she needed to wear a menstrual pad the next day, and she labeled foam "the grossest" because it resulted in even more discharge than any of the suppositories she had used.

Laurie and Wendy complained about the odor created by leaving the sponge in after intercourse. When removed the next morning, each of them found the smell distasteful. Laurie was concerned that the odor she experienced might be due to an allergic reaction to either the spermicide or the material composing the sponge.

Voicing distaste for condom use, Barbara commented, "It's sloppy." Elyse and Nancy described condoms as messy, smelly, and disgusting. Finally, Ivy made a face and remarked, "[they] are ugly when you take them off."

At the age of 18, Maryann chose the diaphragm as her first contraceptive method. She chose it because her mother had used it and found it to be very effective. Initially, insertion was difficult for her, but it became easier after a friend taught her a new way to insert it. She used it consistently for a year and a half and had a problem only once, when the diaphragm tore. Even though she was consistent in its use, she found that after using the diaphragm she felt messy and uncomfortable. She described experiencing a discharge and "goopy" feeling afterward.

Vaginal bleeding was experienced by users of the intrauterine device (IUD) or the pill. Once Kaitlyn had her IUD inserted, she found that "it gave me heavy bleeding." Breakthrough bleeding from the pill was an issue for Mary, Melissa, and Ann. Mary was especially disturbed because the breakthrough bleeding lasted for 21 days of the first month she was on the pill.

Pain and Discomfort

Burning, itching, irritation, or pain were sensations some women experienced each time a contraceptive product was used. The irritating sensations Mary felt when she inserted contraceptive foam and the burning or itching sensations which Kaitlyn experienced with contraceptive suppositories, are possible allergic reactions to the spermicidal products.

When Rose tried the contraceptive sponge, she found it "very uncomfortable." She explained she could feel the "thickness internally and externally." After using it she felt "irritated and itchy from it." Having used both the diaphragm and the sponge, Sandy found the sponge "more comfortable than the diaphragm and the spermicide [in it] isn't as 'goopy.'"

Condoms produced some of the same results. For example, Becky reported the condoms as "uncomfortable" and Elyse "got irritated" when she used them.

The diaphragm was also described as uncomfortable by Maryann. However, she discovered that "learning a new way of inserting it from a friend helped" so it become more comfortable to use. Wendy's description of her use of the diaphragm was that "The pain was unbearable. I had painful cramps with each use. I would double up during the six hours after intercourse that I had to leave it in. When I spoke to the MD about it he said that my body just had to get used to it."

Kaitlyn selected an IUD and then found it "was painful when they put it in." For Sandy, however, once it was inserted she enjoyed the IUD because it was "painless [and I] didn't have to mess with anything and didn't have to worry."

The pill was associated with pain in several ways. For Elyse, using the pill made her breasts bigger so "it really hurts when I walk without a bra." Wendy reported the same experience of "painful breasts." Melissa and Ann experienced headaches, and Ann also experienced "pain in muscles."

Infection

The diaphragm was the cause of bladder infections in both Rose and Kaitlyn. Once Kaitlyn inserted the diaphragm, she "could feel it in there the whole time." In contrast, when Rose used the diaphragm she did not feel any pressure on the bladder, yet she also experienced recurrent infections.

Bodily Changes

After Sharon's IUD was inserted, her stomach became bloated and she had a constant discharge. Other women reported bodily changes which they believed were brought on by using the pill. "That bloaty gross feeling" and weight gain were reported by many women. In addition, some also had what was described by Laurie as complexion problems, or more specifically by Wendy, an increase in acne.

After becoming pregnant, while using condoms for contraception, Jane switched to the pill. She found it unacceptable because it made her "nauseous." This effect was also experienced by Penny.

After Rose started on the pill she gained weight, experienced decreased energy, and maintained the concerns that the hormones were abnormal in her system and that she might develop breast cancer. But she continued to take the pill because there were "no contraptions to fiddle with, so the positive and negative [aspects] weighed out." When she broke up with her partner, she stopped the pill because these aspects "didn't weigh out anymore."

EMOTIONAL RAMIFICATIONS

Oral contraception was the only method reported to cause emotional changes. These emotional ramifications manifested themselves in a variety of ways and ranged from minimal to severe, occurring occasionally or constantly. Some women were afraid that the extent of these emotional changes would drive away their partners.

Negative Changes

When Maryann started taking the pill, she found she experienced mood changes, which she described as "emotional stuff. . . . I was moody, emotionally out of whack, not like myself." The pill's effect on Nancy was that it made her "grumpy and moody," and that it felt like "bad PMS." Rose also experienced "increased PMS symptoms" of being bad tempered. However, Frances said she was "just bitchy." She took the pill because she needed a method with high efficacy, but she "resents Wally [her partner] because I had to go on the pill [and feel this way]."

The pill made Kaitlyn "weepy . . . really emotional." Carol described that "[the pill] made me feel weird, crazy in the head. I tried different types [of pills] but nothing agreed with me." Another effect reported by Wendy was that the pill caused her to have a sense of "depression."

Positive Changes

Not all of the emotional ramifications experienced by women using the pill were considered negative. For example, Melissa enjoyed the effects of the pill for the following reasons: "It evened out my temperament. No more bad mood swings. It decreased the [menstrual] blood flow and the cramps of my period." Using the pill also helped Mary, Paula, and Elaine in the same way. Elaine was relieved to experience "no more periods [lasting] for a full seven days and no more cramps."

The pill provided Ivy with "freedom" for these same reasons. She also enjoyed not having to think about it or worry about having it with her. The use of the pill provided Ivy with what she described as "[a] good guy-bad guy balance. . . . I liked the safety against pregnancy but I was fearful of the hormones and I stayed weepy, very emotional. It bothered me because I felt like I wasn't paying attention to my intuition. It didn't make sense eating health foods and yet, adding hormones to my body."

SEXUAL RAMIFICATIONS

Sometimes the use of a certain method interfered with or enhanced women's sexual experiences. Women identified three areas of concern: spontaneity, continuity, and physical pleasure.

Spontaneity

Condoms were the method mentioned most as interfering with spontaneity. When Wendy used condoms she felt there was "no spontaneity." This was reiterated by Laurie, who did not like condoms because they "affect spontaneity and are not very natural." Ruth found that condoms "decrease spontaneity because (we) had to stop [the act to put it on and then stop again,] too soon before my partner became flaccid. This made it [intercourse] more mechanical."

The sponge was viewed by Laurie as increasing her ability to be spontaneous. She could have it available and use it whenever she desired protected intercourse.

For the same reason, Elyse enjoyed using the pill because it was "easy, convenient, and we could be spontaneous. I can do it [have intercourse] anywhere with no worry."

Continuity

Other women described similar complaints as a lack of continuity. Mary did not like foam because of "stopping to put it in." Withdrawal, stated Nancy, "was terrible. . . . You can't finish what you are doing. It wasn't enjoyable not completing the act."

Mary and Gerri did not like condoms "because of the aggravation of stopping to put it on." Eileen and Elyse did not like the interruption of using condoms. Ann reported that "Condoms seemed to be too much of a hassle. It disrupted us. Several times it almost led us not to use it."

Physical Sensations

Most of the women enjoyed the physical sensations of sexual intercourse and were concerned when they thought the contraceptive measures interfered with their pleasure. Because of past experiences, Wendy disliked withdrawal: "[We] couldn't get an orgasm together because he would pull out for better protection." Foam made Mary too wet and it "decreased sensations" for her.

The use of condoms generated the most comments about decreased physical sensations. Laurie did not "like the feel." Wendy agreed, saying, "[I] don't like the feel and I've tried lubricated, nonlubricated, and all the colors." More specifically, Barbara found that "sometimes they felt dry."

Overall, Ann and Liz did not like the "physical sensations" created by using condoms. Rose said, "[I] thought there was less contact and it decreased sensations. I thought it would feel better without [it]." Nancy reported that it did not feel natural. Ann said, "It didn't feel natural compared to the first time when we didn't use it."

Only Wendy talked about using condoms during oral sex. She found that for her, the use of condoms "makes oral sex disgusting."

CONCERNS FOR PERSONAL SAFETY

Safety concerns expressed by the women ranged from fears of doing permanent damage to their bodies to being unable to retrieve a barrier method after it slipped into the vaginal fornix.

Utilization Difficulties

Women reported difficulties arising during or after the actual use of a contraceptive method. Irma and Carol found that when using condoms they "would slide off." Carol had the experience of having the condom "stuck up in the vagina" and she was afraid she would "lose it inside." Six women–Rose, Irma, Becky, Elyse, Wendy, and Barbara–all reported that condoms broke or ripped during use. Irma thought the condom might have broken because "the foam [she added for extra protection] made the condom weaker."

Laurie reported that the sponge was "hard to keep in." When Sandy, Wendy, and Barbara used it, they had the opposite experience. For Wendy, the biggest difficulty she experienced with the sponge was "getting it out." Providing more detail on her experiences, Sandy reported the sponge would "flip and then I wasn't able to remove it." She had to go to an emergency room to have it removed. Reporting a similar experience, Barbara returned to the Planned Parenthood clinic the next morning to have her sponge removed.

The reverse problem occurred for two women who used an IUD for protection. Both Kaitlyn and Sandy had the experience of having an IUD spontaneously expel, leaving them unprotected against the risk of pregnancy.

The cervical cap also provided difficulties for Ivy, who described her dilemma: "I have short fingers so it is difficult to put it in and take it out." Laughing, and lying on the floor to demonstrate, she said, "I actually writhe on the floor to get it out. I hope I improve with practice."

Concerns About Methods' Effects on the Body

Although they were currently using their selected methods, some women remained concerned about the potential effects on their health and safety. This was true for both the IUD users and the pill users. An IUD user, Sandy worried about damaging her uterus: "At first I worried about perforation of my uterus. Then I figured that since it didn't happen, I was okay."

Other women who expressed fears while continuing to use a method were pill users. Some fears were expressed in generalities such as Paula's comment: "The pill is scary with all the things it can do to your body." Being a little more specific, pill user Ivy explained that she feared dangers to her body with her increasing age and from her continuing habit of smoking.

Other women expressed fears with a specific focus. For Rose, it was a "fear of the danger of breast cancer from using the pill." Ora also feared cancer as well as a heart attack. Reflecting several women's fears, Mary said, "[I] thought that using it [pill] could permanently affect me and make me sterile. I went off the pill when the relationship ended because I feared the dangers [and since the risk of pregnancy had ended]." Fear also caused Laurie to stop the pill when her relationship ended because of her concern about chemicals in her body.

Weighing the Concerns

Both Ivy and Paula were cigarette smokers. They balanced the fear of pregnancy against the increased health risk of smoking while taking the pill. Ivy had a strong need to prevent pregnancy because a previous therapeutic abortion still bothered her. However, she saw no other method options open to her other than the pill, because she had greater fears of the effects of using the IUD.

Other women felt as Maryann did when she talked about "the irony of good [pregnancy protection] versus the evil effect of the ingestion of hormones." She said, "I didn't want to take 'meds' every day, because they were altering my body every day. There were physiological changes and it didn't fit my philosophy." However, she did like the "spontaneity and protection of the pill."

Three other women–Melissa, Liz, and Ruth–reported the same weighing of advantages and disadvantages: effectiveness and convenience of pill against the effects of taking hormones. Each continued using the pill while continually reassessing its use.

CONTENDING WITH USE-EFFECTIVENESS AND THE RISK OF PREGNANCY

Use-effectiveness is defined as the actual effectiveness of a contraceptive method among a particular group of women, taking into account failure to use the method correctly as well as inherent technical failure (Birdsall and Chester, 1987). No matter what method a woman is using or how conscientious she is, she remains aware that pregnancy can occur and keeps a monthly vigil, waiting for the menstrual cycle to begin.

Degree of Concern

The degree of concern that the women experienced while waiting for their menstrual cycles covered a wide range of emotions. Using withdrawal as her method caused what Elyse described as worry: "I worried [about pregnancy] while waiting for my period. I got very nervous when I was late. It really scared me a couple of times." Also using withdrawal, Nancy had the same experience and commented that the waiting "was terrible." The same concern was expressed by Gerri whenever her period was late: "[I] was paranoid about getting pregnant."

Consequences of Concerns

Some women changed their method of protection because of concerns about becoming pregnant or because of the experience of pregnancy. Some, like Paula, chose the pill because they feared "pregnancy and wanted to be 100 percent sure" of prevention. "A concern about pregnancy makes me want better protection," said Frances. As Elyse explained, "My period was late three times while using condoms and withdrawal and each time I was scared that I was pregnant." Searching for more protection she switched to the pill: "It's easier, convenient. I don't want to get scared about being pregnant."

Some women switched to the pill after experiencing a pregnancy. An unintended pregnancy led Carol to switch to the pill: "[It was the] safest so that I wouldn't get pregnant again right away." Jane, Helen, and Wendy began taking the pill after unintended pregnancies because they were told to do so by their health care provider.

Handling Pregnancy

When her menstrual cycle is late, a woman has three options. She may ignore it, do a home test, or seek a pregnancy test at a healthcare facility. If pregnant, her options vary and are determined in part by the reaction of her partner or others if she chooses to tell them about the pregnancy.

Several women spoke about how they had handled the situation when they became pregnant. When Helen did not get her period, she found a provider, went for a pregnancy test, and arranged for an abortion. She did not involve her partner in any of this. After Linda became pregnant, she broke up with her boyfriend and had a therapeutic abortion. Also after becoming pregnant, Mary broke up with her partner, and delivered and cared for the baby alone, until she placed the child up for adoption after a year.

Some women have plans for what they will do if pregnancy occurrs; others have no idea. After a therapeutic abortion, Penny selected the pill as her method although she had experienced side effects when using it in the past. When asked what she would do if the side effects reoccurred, she responded, "Stop." When asked what she would do if she got pregnant again, she responded, "I don't know."

Support from Partners

When Ruth became pregnant, she and her partner went through an abortion together. This type of involvement and support was reported only in long-term relationships.

The prospect of a pregnancy occurring was not an issue that couples readily addressed. Most women, in both long- and short-term relationships, reported that they did not discuss with their partners what would be done if they became pregnant.

An exception was Frances who raised the issue early with her partner: "He said that if something happened he'd be there. We'd get married. But I didn't want to rush into it. You don't get married just because of a baby. [This] concern about pregnancy makes me want better protection."

Support from Others

Sisters and friends were mentioned most often as the support-ive persons to whom these women turned as they made their decisions concerning an unintended pregnancy. Sometimes the male was never aware that the woman had become pregnant.

CONTRACEPTIVE RESPONSES
AFTER UNINTENDED PREGNANCY

Some women stayed with their method even after a pregnancy occurred, maintaining an unrealistic understanding of use-effec-tiveness. After becoming pregnant while using the cap, Eileen continued to use the cap because she "[didn't feel] comfortable with other options. . . . I just thought that if I used it [contracep-tion] I wouldn't get pregnant."

After using suppositories, Kaitlyn said, "I was surprised I became pregnant because I thought that if I were taking care of 'it' I wouldn't get pregnant." After her therapeutic abortion, she again chose suppositories. When a second pregnancy resulted, she switched to the pill.

Switching methods is one way women decrease the strain or worry about pregnancy. Sometimes there is a change to a method with a higher use-effectiveness rate. Other times it is a change to a less efficacious method that, for some reason, a woman feels more confident using. Some women, such as Donna, became pregnant after switching from one pill type to another. After experiencing a therapeutic abortion, Donna gave up the pill and chose the diaphragm.

Some women, such as Connie, abstained for a period of time, ranging from months to years, after experiencing the monthly worry of waiting for their period. Others, such as Linda, switched to abstinence immediately after experiencing an unintended pregnancy.

SUMMARY

Women report many ways in which the use of certain methods affects them. The individual cost and benefit of a contraceptive method, as a woman views it for herself, determines if she continues with a method. (Refer to Table 5.1.) As she weighs the efficacy of the method against the actual ramifications experienced, a decision is reached. She will either maintain consistent use, use the method sporadically, stop use, or change methods. Whichever her choice, the reality of Personalization of Pregnancy Risk can eventually initiate the cycle of considering, choosing, and using a contraceptive over again.

When a woman is fertile and heterosexually active, she becomes aware that her menstrual cycle is an indicator of her pregnancy status. When the scare or actuality of pregnancy occurs, a woman then enters an increased level of consciousness that a pregnancy can happen to her. In handling this phenomenon, a woman reevaluates her contraceptive practice. This revitalized Personalization of Pregnancy Risk starts the cycle of considering, choosing, and using a contraceptive over again. As a result, a woman may decide to maintain her current contracep-

TABLE 5.1. Ramifications of Use of Contraception

Causal Condition	Phenomenon	Context	Intervening Conditions	Actions/Interactions	Consequences
using a contraceptive method properties: –action has been taken –assess effects of use	**Contending with the ramifications of use** –identifies for self the consequences of actions and evaluates the trade-offs	ramifications: physical: intensity: minimal–severe duration: only with use—constant emotional: minimal–severe sexual: minimal–severe relational: minimal–severe	utilization difficulties fears related to side effects and personal safety	weighs efficacy of method against ramifications	uses consistently, uses sporadically, stops use, or changes methods
potential or reality of pregnancy properties: –theoretical effectiveness –actual use of method	**Contending with use effectiveness** –dealing with a monthly concern of unintended pregnancy	monthly concern waiting for menstrual cycle: low–high	perceived support of partner support of others knowledge of options and how to access them	ignores possibility or seeks pregnancy test if pregnant, considers options if not pregnant, reevaluates method, considers method change	changes contraceptive practice changes method, or abstains from intercourse to prevent conception

tive practice, may change her practice, or may abstain from intercourse for a period of time.

CONCLUSIONS

For sexually active women who are at risk for pregnancy, controlling their fertility becomes a recurrent decisional process. The five decision categories are sequential in nature, have a degree of overlap between them, and create a circular process which continues as long as a woman is at risk. The core category, Advocating for Self, evolved as the constant theme linking all five categories and embodied what the fertility regulating phenomenon meant to these women. Preventing pregnancy is only part of women's lives, and is dealt with in a way which attempts to keep it in balance with all other aspects. Advocating for Self describes the fertility regulating process as experienced and described by these women.

REFERENCE

Birdsall, N. and Chester, L. (1987). "Contraception and the status of women: What is the link?" *Family Planning Perspectives,* 19(1), pp. 97-106.

Chapter 6

Women's Stories–Explaining Their Balancing Acts

As women choose and use a contraceptive method, they move through the decisional model of Advocating for Self. Their longitudinal patterns of contraceptive choice and use, as they cycle through the process, often demonstrate a lack of congruence between contraceptive decisions and actual use. Women may use as many as eight different methods and make up to 11 changes as they move back and forth between methods during the contracepting period of their lives (Matteson and Hawkins, 1993). By following the longitudinal development of the contraceptive choices and the explanations of several women, we can become more aware of the concerns and problems they experience when attempting to integrate contraceptive use into their life activities.

KARA

Only 21 years old, Kara's fertility-regulating history provides an example of the conflicting forces she deals with while attempting to control her fertility. Kara describes herself as a third-generation Irish Catholic. Currently she is a full-time college student and works 30 hours per week as a cashier to support herself. She is involved in a steady relationship which includes sexual intercourse. During her four-year history of practicing contraception, Kara has used either male condoms, abstinence, or oral contraception to prevent pregnancy. At this point she is choosing to use condoms and the pill simultaneously.

Kara first became sexually active at the age of 17. By that time she knew of five different ways she could protect herself from pregnancy: abstinence, condoms, spermicidal foam, jelly or creams, and oral contraception. Her sources of information were friends and classes in high school.

For her first episode of intercourse, Kara used male condoms for protection. She chose condoms because they were "easy for [a person] my age to get." She rejected the use of the pill because it was "scary with all the things it can do to you." Kara's partner purchased the condoms from a drugstore and for two years they used them every time they had intercourse. Kara liked using the condom because she "felt protected." Yet, during the two years of use, she maintained a constant "concern that it might not work" and a pregnancy would occur.

Kara believed that both she and her partner maintained a high motivation to prevent pregnancy; yet they never discussed it. They also never discussed what they would do if a pregnancy occurred. She credited her partner with having a positive impact on their responsible contraceptive behavior because he "encouraged the use" of the condom. She never felt it was something she was forcing him to do.

However, her partner let it be known he did not really like using condoms and after two years she finally gave in to his pressure to go on the pill. He told her that he wanted her to use the pill "so that he wouldn't have to worry about bringing condoms." Both felt it would increase their ability for sexual spontaneity.

Despite concerns about the possible long-term effects of the hormones on her body, at age 19, Kara started using oral contraception. With this change, Kara then became the partner completely responsible for contraception. It became her task to seek out a health care provider to obtain the physical and the prescription, purchase her prescription, and then take a pill every day for the next 18 months.

Even though she remained concerned about ingesting it, Kara found using the pill provided her with additional benefits not provided by the use of condoms. She commented, "I didn't have [menstrual] cramps, [my] period was shorter and [I] felt safer against pregnancy." What she did not enjoy was "having to remember to take it every day" and the fact that in order to go on the pill, she had to meet the clinic's requirement "to stop smoking." This cost her a personal pleasure (albeit a healthy move) that her partner did not have to endure.

In actuality then, for Kara's move to using the pill so her boyfriend did not have to remember condoms, the cost to her was: time and expense of a contraceptive gynecological appointment, loss of privacy by admitting she was sexually active, the time and expense of getting the prescription filled, a daily diligence to remember to take the pill correctly, and loss of peace of mind as she worried about the effects of its use. Even though she did all this and provided herself with a higher level of contraceptive efficacy through pill use, she still remained aware she might become pregnant.

After 18 months, Kara stopped using oral contraception because she "transferred schools and lost access to it" at the student health service. She did not go through the effort of investigating a new source because she broke up with her boyfriend and she wanted to start smoking again. During the next year she prevented pregnancy by abstaining from intercourse.

Now at the age of 21, Kara has a relationship which has led to the resumption of intercourse during the last five months. She has resumed the use of condoms for contraceptive protection. She has chosen male condoms because they are "easier and less scary than getting a gynecological (GYN) exam for the pill." She takes the responsibility for obtaining them and buys them at a drugstore. She insists on using them with each act of intercourse and says she likes them because in addition to providing a form of contraception they also protect her against sexually transmitted diseases (STDs). What she does not like is the process of using them: "It was weird having to get used to using it again."

Even though Kara has returned to the use of condoms, she continues to have a "fear of pregnancy." She has addressed that fear by deciding to also return to using the pill. She has chosen to combine the use of condoms and the pill "for the double protection" which she hopes will provide her with a sense of "security."

Returning to the use of oral contraception does not mean that she is entirely comfortable with its use. She said, "When I read all the side effects it really scares me [and] I have to give up smoking again." When asked why she had not chosen another method, she replied, "I can't see myself inserting a diaphragm." She has no plans of exploring any other method choices. Throughout her four years of contraceptive concerns, Kara has found her friends have been the most helpful factor in her success.

Kara's contraceptive activities have not been based on the decision "shall I protect myself or not against pregnancy." While using condoms, she continued to be concerned that she might become pregnant. When she considered using the pill, which has a higher efficacy and should decrease her concerns about the possibility of pregnancy, she became concerned about the effects of the hormones on her body. After these experiences, she advocated for herself, and when again at risk of pregnancy, she chose to use the male condom.

Her contraceptive method choice, which had initially been between a method that caused a concern of increased risk of pregnancy and a method which might cause harm to her body, became more complicated when her partner wanted her to go on the pill. At this time she advocated for herself, by deciding to please him and use the pill. As a result she reaped unexpected benefits, a shorter period with no cramps and reduced concern about pregnancy. However, she became responsible for the contraceptive process and she had to give up smoking.

The decisional balance shifted again for her when she broke up with her partner. Advocating for her self-interests, she went off the pill and resumed smoking. When she resumed intercourse she chose the male condom, thus advocating for herself as she acted on her desire for protection while continuing to smoke. She likes the protection against STDs which condom use provides, and even with her concern of pregnancy, the option on balance was more appealing than the gynecological process necessary to obtain the pill and the prospect of quitting smoking.

Fearful of pregnancy, she is again advocating for herself, this time to reduce her concern of pregnancy and STDs by selecting the pill and the condoms. She is balancing her fears of the pill and the need to give up smoking against her fears of pregnancy and STDs. With her self-knowledge that the insertion of a diaphragm would be a problem for her, she is protecting herself with the only options she perceives to be available to her. Weighing the possibilities of each action, she continues to choose the option which most clearly meets her life needs at the time, thereby continuing to advocate in a holistic manner for herself. Kara's story demonstrates that for her, prevention of pregnancy is only part of her consideration when developing an action plan.

ROSE

Like Kara, Rose also started her contraceptive use with male condoms. Yet during her eight-year history of using contraceptives, assorted considerations have led to very different choices. She has tried five different method options and made six changes since her original method choice.

Rose is an articulate, relaxed, 23-year-old folk singer, currently in a dating relationship which involves sexual intercourse. She knows of seven ways to prevent pregnancy: the cap, male condoms, the diaphragm, foam and condoms, oral contraception, the contraceptive sponge, and withdrawal. She has used all but the cap.

Rose began her sexual activity at the age of 15. During her first encounter she was unprotected because "it was a moment of passion." After that time, she and her partner started using condoms for protection because it involved "the least procedure, no doctor was needed so I didn't need an appointment or anything." Her partner was responsible for buying them, but she did buy them occasionally. They used them about 75 percent of the time for about a year. Rose felt that her partner was even more motivated to prevent pregnancy than she was.

Rose liked using condoms because "it was the thing to do. It made me feel like I was being responsible. [It] was satisfying because I wasn't getting pregnant." However, she thought that "it decreased contact and decreased sensations [and that] it would feel better without it." These thoughts led her to sometimes give greater consideration to her actual sensory experience than to the risk of pregnancy, and she would forgo using them. A difficulty the couple encountered was that the condoms sometimes broke. Several times Rose experimented by adding contraceptive foam to increase the level of protection, but she "didn't like the mess that it created."

After about a year of this activity, Rose became pregnant and chose to have a therapeutic abortion. After recovery, she considered her contraceptive options and chose the diaphragm, which her sister had recommended to her about two years earlier. She liked this choice because she "felt more in control." She explained that she felt "safer, more secure [against pregnancy and] like I was taking more personal responsibility." Obtaining the diaphragm from a clinic, she and her partner divided the cost of use. With the decision to use the diaphragm, Rose advocated for herself by choosing a method with higher efficacy while maintaining her sensory experience during intercourse. The idea of using the diaphragm pleased her and she increased her consistency of contraceptive use to 85 percent.

Her use remained less than 100 percent because with continued use Rose found the diaphragm was uncomfortable and she had recurrent bladder infections. Rose explained that because of this discomfort, "sometimes I just didn't choose to use it." Each time she moved toward the possibility of intercourse she had to decide whether or not to use protection. Her choices were either to have unprotected intercourse with the inherent possibility of a pregnancy occurring; or, to decrease her risk through the use of the diaphragm, with the resulting uncomfortableness during intercourse and the possibility of a bladder infection. The repeated occurrence of bladder infections led her to advocate for herself and decrease diaphragm use. Then, fearful of pregnancy, she reconsidered her contraceptive options again. Her mother accompanied her to a birth control clinic and urged her to use the pill.

At age 18, with a serious boyfriend and the anticipation of frequent intercourse, she decided to go on oral contraception. Rose remembered to take the pill about 95 percent of the time. She enjoyed using the pill because there were "no contraptions to fiddle with." Her partner was supportive, reminding her to take it, splitting the cost of the pill and using condoms when she missed pills. With this cooperation, the pill remained her method of choice for two years.

As expected, using the pill was not without personal costs. Rose felt "uncomfortable about having something artificial in my system." She gained weight and became less energetic. However, these difficulties did not decrease her consistency in use because "the positives and negatives weighed out."

When Rose was 20, the relationship with this boyfriend broke up. Since she was not having intercourse, the fear of continued hormone use led her to advocate for her health and to stop taking oral contraception. As she stated, "the positives and negatives didn't weigh out anymore." Her specific concerns were: "Sometimes women develop breast cancer and it frightened me that I was on the pill [so] I stopped taking it because I wasn't in a steady relationship."

During the next two years, Rose had intercourse a few times. For pregnancy protection she "experimented with the contraceptive sponge" which she purchased at the drugstore. However, she did not like it because it was "very uncomfortable, felt too thick," she could feel it when it was in, it caused irritation, and made her itchy. Her dissatisfaction eventually led her to stop using it.

Now at the age of 23, she has obtained a new diaphragm. During use she feels no pressure on her bladder and no bladder infections have occurred. She has felt comfortable enough that she has used it 100 percent of the time when she has had intercourse. However, another unplanned pregnancy occurred and has been resolved with a therapeutic abortion. Now, Rose has begun to feel that using the diaphragm is not enough. She thinks she would feel safer, not only from pregnancy but also from AIDS and other STDs, if she used condoms with the diaphragm. At this time, Rose has chosen not to return to the pill because of the way it has made her feel in the past. She sees her decisions on contraception as trying to "balance (my) health between large doses of hormones and the risk of pregnancy."

PENNY

Penny believes that oral contraception is the best protection against pregnancy. During the last few years, she has tried repeatedly to balance successfully its use with a level of personal comfort. After five starts with oral contraception and a therapeutic abortion, she will now use male condoms and vaginal film until she can complete a new cycle of oral contraception.

Penny is a 25-year-old bank teller. At the age of 20, she chose to protect herself with oral contraception before her first act of intercourse. She chose this method over the other five options she was aware of: the intrauterine device (IUD), vaginal film, male condoms, diaphragm, and sponge. She learned about these options from her friends. Throughout her five years of contracepting she has chosen to use either the pill or condoms for protection. Her history of method use demonstrates her desire to use methods with the highest efficacy levels, although the effects of the pill have caused discomfort to her physical well-being.

When Penny chose the pill, she did not know exactly what to expect, but she felt she "should do something before (I) got pregnant." She obtained the pill on her own and used it consistently while she was having intercourse two times a week. She liked using it because she "didn't worry about getting pregnant."

What she did not anticipate were the side effects she experienced. She described a "bloaty, gross feeling and nausea," which led her to stop the pill after two months. She then continued to have intercourse, but without any contraceptive protection. An unplanned pregnancy occurred followed by a therapeutic abortion. As Penny explained, "Going off the pill made me get pregnant the last time. I didn't think I had as big a chance of getting pregnant if I used nothing. Since I have done it so much without anything and I didn't get pregnant, I figured I wouldn't." Penny then returned to the use of the pill, but a different brand. She hoped that the new type of pill would have less dramatic physical effects for her.

Again after two months of use, she chose to stop taking the pill because she felt terrible while on it. When she discussed this with her partner, he supported her in stopping its use. He supported the fact that she "shouldn't be on it if she doesn't like it." For protection they chose condoms; however, her partner found these bothered him so they were used only occasionally.

Afraid of a repeat pregnancy, she went back on the pill, but again was able to tolerate its effects for only two months. Angry with what it was doing to her body, she again quit. "I can't stand not being able to button my pants," she said in reference to the bloating she experienced. This became a pattern of starting and then stopping contraceptive use, which repeated itself over and over. Fear of pregnancy drove her to take the pill, and then concern about the changes it created in her body led her to stop taking it. Penny feels as if she has been "off and on [the pill] a thousand times."

Afraid of the occurrence of another pregnancy, with this gynecological visit she is considering the use of condoms and vaginal film. In the meantime, she continues to have unprotected intercourse at a rate averaging eight times per month. If she gets pregnant, she does not have a clue as to what she will do.

When asked why she does not consider any other methods available to her, she responded that she does not like the idea of the IUD because she fears infection. She has rejected the use of the barrier methods of sponge and diaphragm because of concerns about inserting and removing them.

Penny felt that she went off the pill "for selfish reasons," and said, "If I don't like how I feel, I say forget it." In the future, she anticipates that "like a jerk" she will return again to the use of oral contraception. When asked if she thought it would be okay, she responded, "I don't know, we'll see. If it has side effects, I stop. I don't know what I'll do if I get pregnant."

Penny continues to experience a great deal of difficulty in balancing the need for pregnancy protection with the desire to feel physically well. She continues to try to find the balance between the need for protection from a "risk of pregnancy" and the actual effects her body experiences when she takes the pill.

As she prepared to leave the interview, Penny became pensive and then offered, "My parents would freak if they ever knew [I was on the pill]. I have to hide the pills and everything from them." With this statement she added other factors to the balancing act she has been attempting to solve. At first it appeared to be just between the risk of pregnancy and her body's negative response to the pill. Now, these other factors that have emerged–that at 25, she must hide signs of contraceptive use from her parents, and that she lacks the sanction of her parents for her sexual activity–are made apparent in her equation of consideration.

SUMMARY

Kara, Rose, and Penny have each faced the same risk and made different choices. Like millions of other women, each have faced the issue of decreasing their risk of pregnancy by using different forms of contraception. (Refer to Table 6.1.) Only Kara has remained pregnancy free. The process of thinking about and then acting on the decision to use contraceptives has not been free of turmoil for these women, as they have moved through the decisional model of Advocating for Self. Whether starting with the use of condoms and then choosing methods with increasing levels of efficacy, or by trying repeatedly to work oral contraception into her life in an acceptable manner, each woman has tried repeatedly to balance her choice of contraceptive method against the risk of pregnancy. These women's histories of contraception are not unusual. Each points out the difficulties some women experience in attempting to successfully integrate contraceptive use into their lives, and the reasons they repeatedly return to Advocating for Self.

REFERENCE

Matteson, P. and Hawkins, J. (1993). "What family planning methods women use and why they change them," *Health Care for Women International,* 14(6), pp. 539-548.

TABLE 6.1. Patterns of Choice

Kara:	condoms	→ pill	→ condoms	→ condoms and pill			
Rose:	condoms →	foam and condoms →	diaphragm →		→ pill	→ diaphragm →	
	sponge →	diaphragm →					
Penny:	pill →	nothing →	pill	nothing →	pill	→ pill →	nothing
	pill →	nothing →	pill	nothing →	condoms & contraceptive film →		anticipates starting pill use again within the month

Chapter 7

A New Perspective–Advocating for Self

Women of today are choosing contraceptive methods in a manner different from that attributed to women in the past. As described by the substantive theory, Advocating for Self, they are making decisions about contraception based on the complexity of their life needs. Women demonstrate contraceptive decision-making strategies which do not follow the mathematical models of statisticians and economists (Resnik, 1987) or the rational, prescriptive model described by Janis and Mann (1977). They are instead subjective, relational decisions as described by the psychological theorist Gilligan (1982).

This dissimilarity is expected because "given the differences in women's conception of self and morality, women bring to the lifecycle a different point of view and order human experience in terms of different priorities" than men (Gilligan, 1982, p. 22). "Sensitivity to the needs of others and the assumption of responsibility for taking care, lead women to attend to voices other than their own and to include in their judgment other points of view" (Gilligan, 1982, p. 16).

THE THEORY OF ADVOCATING FOR SELF

Controlling one's fertility is a process as individualized as the participants themselves. However, certain aspects of decision making about fertility regulation are common to many women's experiences.

When the capacity for pregnancy becomes a factor in a woman's life, her view of the actual potential determines how she responds. If she desires to prevent pregnancy she will respond differently than if she desires pregnancy. Most women desire to control their fertility and prevent pregnancy for portions, if not all, of their fertile years. When attempting to gain control they sometimes seek the assistance of a health care professional.

A woman's feelings concerning contraception develop in response to her interactions with others regarding this activity. Women consider the views of others as well as their other life obligations when making a contraceptive choice. Women garner the opinions of society in general, as well as those of family, friends, significant others, and health care professionals concerning why and how they should control their fertility. Sources of contraceptive information which women find helpful are books, classes, magazines, the media, friends and family. (It was notable that health care providers were not prominent in the memories of the women in the study group).

The meaning each woman attaches to the activity of regulating her fertility is handled in, and modified through, various interpretive processes. Using contraceptive options, sometimes in sequential attempts to control their fertility, women do not always choose and continuously use the most efficacious pregnancy preventing method available to them. Most women carefully change from one method to another, in a pattern of selection which may decrease the efficacy of their pregnancy protection but which will benefit them in some other way.

After realizing that she is at risk of pregnancy, a woman identifies how this prospect impacts with other factors in her life. These thoughts guide her actions related to choice and use of fertility regulating methods. The desire to prevent pregnancy is the force which motivates a woman to consider the use of contraception and its possible effects on her life. Determining the impact using contraception will have on the other aspects of her life guides her decisions as she chooses and then uses one or more fertility regulating options.

A woman attempts to prevent pregnancy after considering what she perceives to be the risks associated with her use of contraceptive options. With the implementation of a fertility regulation method, two potential health "problems" remain: an unintended pregnancy, and the side effects/dangers of contraceptive methods. While experiencing a pregnancy is a far more risky health problem than contracepting, most contraceptive methods have side effects and some pose the possibilities of life-threatening dangers. With implementation of use, a woman may experience risks to her physical, emotional, sexual, and/or relational well-being. (Some partners will beat or leave a woman if they discover she is using contraceptives.) These experiences may cause her to reevaluate the balance between her personal risk of pregnancy and her personal risks as a consequence of practicing contraception.

INFLUENCES OF PARTNERS

A woman considers the views of others, including her current partner, in choosing a contraceptive method to use. When a partner dislikes a particular method, the woman often takes on the quest of trying to find a product which would satisfy both their needs. Women combine concern for others with a sense of obligation and sacrifice, as well as with sensitivity to avoid hurting others (Gilligan, 1982). Women are willing to put up with methods which are less than desirous to them–such as an IUD, diaphragm, or the pill–rather than risk offending their partners.

In contrast, women report that their partners are generally more concerned with their own sexual satisfaction than contraception. This is not surprising, as the burden of an undesired pregnancy is borne by the female whether abortion or birth is the eventual course of action.

"As soon as some women think of incurring someone else's displeasure–especially a man's–they equate it with [possible] abandonment" (Miller, 1976, p. 110). For a woman, being alone is often one of the greatest and most frightening threats she may face, so it overshadows any risk of the occurrence of an unintended pregnancy (Miller, 1976). It is only when a woman can move away from thinking of first pleasing her partner and conforming to his desires and expectations that she can start to consider acting on her own needs. This explains why, when Advocating for Self, some women have weighed their dislike of a method against their partners' preference in contraceptive matters and have given priority to the pleasure of their partners within the decisional equation. Health care providers have the opportunity to explore with a woman her personal contraceptive desires and to support her in working toward her preferences.

INTERACTIONS WITH HEALTH CARE PROVIDERS

Women report that health care providers teach them how to initiate a new contraceptive method but do little, if any, problem solving to address obstacles which may interfere with their continued use (Matteson and Hawkins, 1993). This type of care has not resulted in the consistent achievement of fertility regulation by all clients desiring to prevent pregnancy (Jones et al., 1988; Oakley, Denyes, and O'Connor, 1989). Some women never use the method they choose and others change methods after a short period of time. As a result, many women switch methods or discontinue use in the first year following the clinic visit (Oakley, Sereika, and Bogue, 1991).

Some "women experience themselves as mindless and voiceless and subject to the whims of external authority" (Belenky et al., 1986, p. 15). When a person in authority, such as a health care worker, implies or directly tells a woman that a specific method is the one she should be using, she will eventually agree with the provider, at least while she remains within the provider's domain–the office or examination room. Belenky explains that "girls and women have more difficulty than boys and men in asserting their authority or considering themselves as authorities" even when it comes to their personal preferences (Belenky et al., 1986, p. 4-5). So a woman will agree with the authority figure and accept the contraceptive solution provided, without exploring how the implementation of use relates to life experience.

Once away from the care provider "authority figure," a woman will attempt to maintain her subjective knowledge and to protect a space for growth and maintenance of self (Belenky et al., 1986). Instead of following the professional's directions, she will integrate the knowledge which she intuitively felt was important with the knowledge learned from others, creating a more complete, personally "constructed knowledge." With a combination of rational and emotive thought and objective and subjective knowing, a woman makes a decision about how she will proceed with the contraceptive option the professional has provided (Belenky et al., 1986, p. 134). She may choose to attempt to use the method, but she will only be successful in developing a pattern of consistent use if this action continues to agree with her intuitive self and may be integrated into her lifestyle.

EMPOWERING WOMEN

Women have a fundamental desire to take control and responsibility for contraceptive decisions in their lives. Once they see themselves as capable of making a contraceptive choice, they are able to feel responsible for themselves in this area of their lives. To take on this independent activity, women need to delineate in their own terms, the experiences of their adult lives (Gilligan, 1982).

"Conflicts between health care professionals and patients are not uncommon, . . . there is tension between what the patient wants and what the professional believes the patient needs"

(Childress, 1982, p. 3). In a paternalistic model of care, health care providers make all the decisions for clients, including what self-care will be taught and what care options will be offered. Health care providers justify this "power over" philosophy by contending that because of their training they know what is best for the individual woman (Bille, 1987; Lind, Wilburn, and Pate, 1986). This model of care not only supports a stereotype of women as inferior, compliant, and passive, but requires it (Andrist, 1988). Contraceptive programs, developed on this paternalistic, medical model respond not to the situation as experienced by the woman, but to the institutionalized needs and beliefs of the care providers (Luker, 1975). Women find family planning programs do not address their concerns and help them become successful in implementing a plan of care. The usual care in family planning settings does not include an assessment of women's abilities to carry out the repetitive and complex actions required for optimal use-effectiveness of fertility regulation methods (Dodge and Oakley, 1989). Reluctant to return for follow-up care, women move to over-the-counter methods and try to solve the problem of pregnancy risk with the assistance of their friends and sometimes their partners. Women who are unable to implement the provider-directed method of care are labeled with the erroneous term of noncompliant. In fact what has happened is that the health care provider has been nonhelpful to specific women's needs.

Many of the erroneous assumptions about women and their use of contraception, referred to in the first chapter of this book, have arisen because of philosophical differences between the paternalistic providers and the female consumers. Many care providers approach the issue of fertility regulation from a limited and pragmatic view. In essence, if a woman does not want to get pregnant, she uses "the best method," the method with the highest efficacy. If for whatever reason a woman does not use the best method, then she must want to get pregnant, even if she does not know it. This paternalistic model disregards consideration of a woman's personal values or lifestyle.

In contrast, health care programs developed on a "power-from-within" philosophy provide a more horizontal structure of information exchange and decision-making responsibilities (Lind, Wilburn, and Pate, 1986). With a woman-centered model, care providers are able to acknowledge and respond to a woman's interconnectedness with others in her family and support system. They assist and support her desire for self-determination by exploring with her the full range of available options and how each could be successfully integrated as a component with the rest of her life.

Most women are not making their contraceptive decisions based on the rational, prescriptive perspective. Therefore, care based exclusively on this approach must be changed to provide support for the relational issues in a woman's decisions. It is only then that the full complexity of women's fertility regulating decisions may be addressed in a more appropriate and supportive manner.

A woman can reduce the number of unintended pregnancies she experiences only with consistent and correct use of contraceptive methods. But, consistent and correct use may only occur after she successfully integrates the regimen of use into her already established patterns of daily life. Attempts to reconstruct these patterns around contraceptive activity are not generally adaptable in the long term. To assist in a woman's success, care providers must address individual needs by listening to the different voices of women.

PROVIDING APPROPRIATE CONTRACEPTIVE CARE

Women's contraceptive behaviors are complex, often reflecting considerable dissonance between intention and behavior (Oakley, Sereika, and Bogue, 1991). Essential health care for women must become holistic, rather than maintain its current provider focus (Andrist, 1988). Appropriate contraceptive care is essential to the health and well-being of women.

Unfortunately, a holistic understanding of women's contraceptive patterns and processes is just beginning to be developed. Women, across a broad spectrum of age, racial, social, and economic groups, acknowledge the various factors in their lives which affect their patterns of contraceptive use. They explain the processes and factors which led them to seek, choose, and then use a fertility regulating method.

Experiences in other areas of health care have demonstrated that just providing information about healthy behavior to a client does not necessarily produce that behavior. More specifically, when women's expectations surrounding health care interventions have not been met, the result is a lower sense of satisfaction and decreased compliance with the directed interventions. Gaining an understanding of the influences of fertility regulating patterns from the client's perspective is the first step in developing interventions which offer congruence between the needs of women and the care they currently receive. In order to accomplish this, the following three areas need to be addressed in practice.

First. Much of the care provided to women today is based on a patriarchal system in which the woman is told what to do. If she questions or refuses, she is often labeled as noncompliant. Even when receiving care from a woman, the training, expectations and protocols of intervention are often based on the patriarchal model of rational, prescriptive decision making, rather than a woman-centered model allowing for subjective, relational decision making. Changing this model in order to offer appropriate care requires the identification and rejection of a practice based on "the traditional [patriarchal] medical model in favor of one generally concerned with attaining, retaining, and regaining health" however the woman defines it (McBride and McBride, 1981, p. 41). Because the locus of contraceptive control justly belongs to the female client, this adjusted approach will more reliably meet her contraceptive decision-making needs and enhance the possibility of success.

Second. In order to maintain control of their life choices, women desire to control their fertility. But for many women the decision whether to use a birth control method is more complex than a decision to prevent pregnancy or attempt pregnancy when sexually active. Women express broader considerations such as: personal health concerns, both immediate and long term; the effects on the relationship; and the quality of the sexual interaction itself. These issues sometimes lead women to forgo contraception even when they want to avoid pregnancy.

Also, a woman may desire sexual activity and want to avoid pregnancy, yet finds she is not able to meet both these desires without worrying about or interfering with her overall sense of health or well-being. The conflicting concerns which women experience while attempting to integrate fertility regulation into their lives need to be addressed in a holistic manner, because "if you only see part of a person, you will only treat part of a person" (McBride and McBride, 1981, p. 47).

Third. In describing what she would develop as the perfect birth control method, each woman defines in effect what the basic criteria are as she chooses and then sometimes changes methods. The terms: convenient (something in the water), reliable (would not be worrying all the time if it worked), reversible (take a pill to counteract), and safe (no health hazards) summarize these descriptions. These are the factors–convenient, reliable, reversible, and safe–which must be addressed by providers when a woman is attempting to choose and integrate a method of fertility regulation into her lifestyle. Determining what each of these terms means to a woman with regard to fertility regulation, and how she would priortize them within her particular life situation, is an important step toward meaningful care.

To fulfill this need, the provider must take the time and have the ability to discuss sexual practices comfortably and openly, not with a broad or hypothetical focus, but with a sense of the woman's reality. The provider must then collaborate with the woman as she explores how to actually integrate the use of a specific method when she is initially choosing or later changing contraception.

Women want assistance in the exploration of specific areas of concern when they are starting a contraceptive method new to them. These areas include: maintaining easy access, covering the financial expense of use, her own and partner's comfort level during use, establishing a cadre of people supportive of her effective use, and knowledge of back-up methods of protection. (Refer to Appendix E for more details.) Efforts to explore these areas will help to increase the frequency and longevity of the utilization of her choice. Future models of contraceptive care must recognize the wisdom of actively involving clients in the process, with the professional and client actively collaborating in a holistic assessment of the client's needs and developing a realistic plan for meeting them.

The theory of Advocating for Self provides an explanation of women's contraceptive challenges as related by women themselves. It fosters understanding of the human health-related experience of women seeking fertility regulation, provides an expanded awareness of the interrelationship between women and their environments with regard to this health issue, identifies a substantive theory of women's fertility decision-making processes, and provides a conceptual model through which providers can more effectively guide the care of women who use contraceptives.

REFERENCES

Andrist, L. (1988). "A feminist framework for graduate education in women's health." *Journal of Nursing Education*, 27(2), pp. 66-70.

Belenky, M. F., Clinchy, B., Goldberger, N., and Tarule, J. (1986). *Women's way of knowing*. New York: Basic Books, Inc.

Bille, D. (1987). "Locus of decision making in patient and family education: Its effect on promoting wellness." *Nursing Administration Quarterly*, 11(3), pp. 62-65.

Childress, J. (1982). *Who should decide? Paternalism in health care*. New York: Oxford Press.

Dodge, J. and Oakley, D. (1989). "Analyzing nurse-client interactions in family planning clinics." *Journal of Community Health*, 6, pp. 37-44.

Gilligan, C. (1982). *In a different voice*. Cambridge, MA: Harvard University Press.

Janis, I., and Mann, L. (1977). *Decision making*. New York: The Free Press.

Jones, E. F., Forrest, J. D., Henshaw, S. K., Silverman, J., and Torres, A. (1988). "Unintended pregnancy, contraceptive practice and family planning services in developed countries." *Family Planning Perspectives*, 20(2), pp. 53-67.

Lind, A., Wilburn, S., and Pate, E. (1986). "Power-from-within: Feminism and the ethical decision-making process in nursing." *Nursing Administration Quarterly*, 10(3), pp. 50-57.

Luker, K. (1975). *Taking chances: Abortion and the decision not to contracept*. Berkeley, CA: University of California Press.

Matteson, P. and Hawkins, J. (1993). "What family planning methods women use and why they change them." *Health Care for Women International*, 14(6), pp. 539-548.

McBride, A. and McBride, W. (1981). "Theoretical underpinnings for women's health." *Women and Health*, 6(1/2), pp. 37-55.

Miller, J. (1976). *Toward a new psychology of women*. Boston, MA: Beacon Press.

Oakley, D., Denyes, M. J., and O'Connor, N. (1989). "Expanded nursing care for contraceptive use." *Applied Nursing Research*, 2, pp. 121-127.

Oakley, D., Sereika, S., and Bogue, E. (1991). "Oral contraceptive pill use after an initial visit to a family planning clinic." *Family Planning Perspectives*, 20, pp. 150-154.

Resnik, M. (1987). *Choices–An introduction to decision theory*. Minneapolis, MN: University of Minnesota Press.

Appendix A
Definition of Terms

client: a female who seeks professional assistance with fertility regulation.

contraceptive failure: when conception occurs during a period of contraceptive method use.

fertility control methods: one of the following methods of contraception listed by respondents: oral contraception, intrauterine device, diaphragm, cervical cap, spermicidal foam, jelly, cream, film or vaginal suppository, condom, sponge, natural family planning, withdrawal, abstinence, and surgical sterilization.

fertility regulation: the use of one or more methods designed to inhibit the capacity to conceive a pregnancy.

health care provider: a professional educated as an obstetrical/ gynecological nurse practitioner, physician, or family planning counselor.

theoretical effectiveness: the effect of a contraceptive under ideal laboratory conditions. It depends solely on the method and is not affected by human error.

unintended pregnancy: classified as such if at the time of conception the woman had stopped, or had not used, contraception for reasons other than seeking pregnancy; or the woman had become pregnant while using contraception.

use-effectiveness: measures the protection from unintended pregnancy under real-life use conditions, allowing for user's carelessness or error as well as method failures.

Appendix B
Genesis of the Study

PURPOSE

The purpose of this investigation was to determine women's perceptions of the dynamic process of fertility regulation by exploring, from the perspective of women who desire to use contraceptives, the factors that have influenced their patterns of contraception. This research intended to uncover the contraceptive needs, interests, and experiences of these selected women. It was expected that developing a holistic understanding of this experience from the perspectives of women could reveal descriptions of factors which influence their various patterns of behavior. Extending the knowledge base with these insights could lead to the development of a paradigm explaining the interrelatedness of factors. With this new understanding, interventions to improve women's lives could be developed, thereby increasing congruence between the actual needs of women and the contraceptive care they receive.

RESEARCH QUESTIONS

The following descriptive questions comprised the core of this study: What are women's strategies for managing their fertility? What factors influence women's fertility regulating experiences?

LIMITATIONS OF THE STUDY

This study is not generalizable to other populations due to the methodological design and the limitations of the population.

Some of the identified limitations of the sample of respondents are that they are limited to women who:

1. have found accessible sources of care and supplies
2. have chosen to interact with health care providers
3. have chosen to utilize at least one method
4. are a mix of races but it is unknown if it is in the same proportion as the clinic population or is reflective of the community
5. are all English-speaking.

LITERATURE REVIEW

The literature is replete with information concerning women and their fertility regulation. Most of the research, aggregate in nature, is based on statistical analysis of large data bases developed from questionnaires or interviews conducted on a national level. Many of the quests for defining variables have resulted from societal conjecture about women and their circumstances. Major assumptions have been that unintended pregnancies occur because women are ignorant about methods, are unaccepting of their own sexuality, lack access to care, have irrational fears about specific contraceptives, maintain conflicting attitudes and beliefs about birth control, and/or are unable to be logical about the linkage between unprotected intercourse and conception (Gerrard, McCann, and Geis, 1984).

Survey Studies

In an attempt to obtain the data from the women themselves, the National Center for Health Statistics conducted the National Survey of Family Growth in 1973 (Cycle I), 1976 (Cycle II), 1982 (Cycle III), and 1988 (Cycle IV). The personal interviews, averaging about an hour in length, provide "information on a number of topics related to childbearing, family planning, and related aspects of maternal and child health" (Mosher and Pratt, 1990, p. 2). Cycle I had 9,797 respondents and Cycle II had 8,611 respondents, all never-married women or single women living in the same home as their children. Single women without children or living apart from their children were not included. Cycle III with 7,979 respondents and Cycle IV with 8,450 respondents broadened their sample base by including single women (Hammerslough, 1984). Each of these surveys has produced data which many researchers have used to explore various aspects of fertility regulation. The following reports are concerned with women's discontinuation of methods or method switching based on one or more of these surveys.

Using the combined data from Cycles I and II of the National Survey of Family Growth (NSFG), Grady et al., (1983) analyzed the method continuation rates for the period July 1, 1970 through December 31, 1975. They found that the pill and IUD had high proportions of users discontinuing use for method-related reasons other than unintended pregnancy (25.9 percent and 21.4 percent, respectively).

Hammerslough (1984) examined the abandonment of all methods for reasons other than to become pregnant or to switch methods. With an analysis that allowed the simultaneous consideration of many variables, he found that the significant indicators of improper use were: age at beginning of contracepting interval, race, education, contraceptive method being used, duration of use, parity, poverty, and religion. He defined improper use of a method as anything on a continuum from occasional lapses to outright discontinuation. He speculated that "discontinuation is probably a tip-of-the-iceberg indicator of a higher indicator of improper use" (Hammerslough, 1984, p. 18). When married and separated women were compared, Bumpass and Rindfuss (1984) found that the patterns of contraceptive-use behavior were very similar when the separated women remained sexually active.

Data from the 1982 NSFG, which interviewed single women, determined that most women use more than one type of contraceptive method in the course of their childbearing years. "Among all those who have ever practiced contraception, the average number of methods is 2.8" (Forrest, 1987, p. 133). In contrast, the married women aged 15 to 44 years reported an average of 1.09 methods used and a high proportion of discontinuation with adoption of no method. About half of the women who discontinued their method during the first year of use did not immediately adopt another method type (Grady, Hayward, and Florey, 1988). When former users of the pill were isolated, these researchers found that most users had quit due to some physical problem. Their next choices were sterilization (21 percent), a nonpermanent method (60 percent), or no method (19 percent). Half of the pill quitters adopted a new method without any break in contraceptive practice, 20 percent had a break in use but were not exposed to the risk of unintended pregnancy, and 27 percent were exposed to pregnancy risk but went unprotected for some time after they quit using the pill. These method changes suggest "that the decline in pill use was driven largely by the perceived disadvantages of the pill, rather than by the attractions of other methods" (Pratt and Bachrach, 1987, p. 265). However, since the women were not asked their reasons for their next selection, it remains speculation.

A comparison between Cycle III in 1982 and Cycle IV in 1988 revealed that in those six years, the sample as a whole changed its methods of fertility regulation. The percent of those using female sterilization as a method of contraception increased from 23 to 28 percent. At the same time the proportion using the pill rose from 28 percent to 31 percent, the proportion using the condom increased from 12 percent to 15 percent, and the proportion using the IUD dropped sharply, from 7 percent to 2 percent (Mosher and Pratt, 1990).

Another recurrent survey has also been used to provide data for analysis concerning women's patterns of method usage. The survey, which has been commissioned annually for almost two decades by Ortho, is a short, self-administered questionnaire that asks women about their contraceptive use and attitudes (Forrest and Fordyce, 1988). In the spring of 1982, the survey was mailed to 6,500 married and 3,500 unmarried women aged 18 to 44 in families of an ongoing panel sample. Seventy-seven percent of the married women and 50 percent of the unmarried women answered the questionnaire.

A woman's "plans to change her current method and her choice of a future method, are, to some extent, an indication of levels of satisfaction or dissatisfaction with available methods" (Forrest and Henshaw, 1983, p. 158). In this survey, women using nonprescription methods (withdrawal, condoms, rhythm, and foam) were more likely to be considering a change in methods than those using prescription methods (the pill, the IUD, and the diaphragm) (Forrest and Henshaw, 1983). Since only women's current methods were obtained, data on sequential patterns of usage were not available. The 1987 survey of this Ortho series revealed that, "the average number of methods reported per user was 1.17. This was just slightly higher than the 1.13 average reported in the same survey in 1982" (Forrest and Fordyce, 1988). However, both of these figures are much lower than the ones obtained by the National Survey of Family Growth. Perhaps the difference in the lower aspect of the age range contributed to this (NSFG–15 to 44; Ortho–18 to 44).

Zelnick, Koenig, and Kim (1984), using data from a national probability sample survey of women aged 15 to 19, living in households in metropolitan areas in the contiguous United States, found that 40 percent of teenage women used a prescription contraceptive as their first contraceptive method. Of all who had been sexually active before using the prescription method, 80 percent of the whites and 50 percent of the blacks had previously used a nonprescription method. Further results concerning method sequencing are limited because the "survey included questions on dates of first and second intercourse (and last intercourse), as well as on dates of first and last use and nonuse of contraceptives, but did not attempt to obtain a complete sexual history" (Zelnick, Koenig, and Kim, 1984, p. 10).

Other researchers have explored the discontinuation of specific methods. Krishnamoni and Jain (1985) reported that during the first year of use, "approximately 30 percent of women choosing the pill and 15 percent of women choosing the intrauterine device give them up. The side effects of the oral contraceptive or intrauterine device appear to be a major factor in the discontinuation of birth control" (Krishnamoni and Jain, 1985, p. 96). "Many individuals tend to lose confidence in a method they have been using success-fully or fear its consequences for their health" (Ory, Forrest, and Lincoln, 1983, p. 4). Usually no more than 50 to 70 percent of women who start the pill are still using it one year later (Hatcher et al., 1986). Only 58 percent of a sample of 237 college females reported continuous usage of the pill with no breaks. Of the women who discontinued the pill, 29.1 percent reported one restart on the pill, 8.7 percent reported two restarts, and 3.9 percent indicated three restarts (Sawyer and Beck, 1989). When users give up the pill they may switch to a less effective method or, perhaps temporarily, risk pregnancy by using no method while pondering what to do (Ory, Forrest, and Lincoln, 1983).

The estimates of method use derived from these surveys are important from an epidemiological perspective, as national trends are revealed. However, there are limitations as these surveys pro-vide data only as to what women are using at a particular point in time and then compare aggregate patterns of use to previous ag-gregate data. Individual patterns of choice and change are not addressed (Forrest and Fordyce, 1988).

QUALITATIVE STUDIES

Rather than deal with aggregate data, other researchers have utilized different methodological techniques to determine the indi-vidual patterns of contraceptive users. Utilizing grounded theory methodology, Lindemann (1972) developed a theory of contraceptive method sequencing. The data were collected from May 1968 through December 1970, by interviewing 102 mostly unmarried women from the ages of 13 to 26. Based on these data, the Prescription Process was developed, which describes a three-step pattern of birth control choices for the young women in this sample.

The first step was labeled the natural stage, the "do nothing" stage. The second step, or peer prescription stage, is described thus: after discussion with friends and experimenting, women chose rhythm, withdrawal, foam, condoms, or the douche (Lindemann, 1972). Lindemann asserts that women move to the "expert stage" when they are ready to disclose sexual activity to an expert in order to obtain the most effective means of avoiding pregnancy: pills, IUD, diaphragm, or abortion. Lindemann thus proposes that women tend to upgrade their practice of contraception in stages from nonuse, to use of nonexpert, to use of a method supplied by an expert. She developed a linear model to demonstrate this movement. What she failed to explain was the regression that many of her respondents demonstrated. At the time of report, 20 percent (n = 20) of the women had regressed in stages, 17 percent (n = 17) had not yet left the natural stage, and 16 percent (n = 16) had returned to it.

In 1976, Miller reported on women's method sequencing in a descriptive study with data collected prior to 1971. He compared two groups of single, sexually active women, half of whom had never been pregnant (n = 26) and half of whom had just recently confirmed an unwanted pregnancy (n = 26) and were applying for an abortion. All the women were Caucasian, varied in age from 17 to 26, had never married, and had not been pregnant previously. Utilizing a series of unstructured interviews with a focus on sexuality and contraception from early adolescence to the time of the study, Miller found what he termed "a natural sequencing of contraceptive behavior" among these women, as they changed from one method to the next. He reported that "typically they began with

the use of abstinence itself, periodic abstinence or rhythm and withdrawal or what may be called partial abstinence" (Miller, 1976).
The subsequent methods were coitus-dependent methods: foam
and/or condoms. The third choice was the use of prescription methods: oral contraception or the diaphragm. None of the women in
this sample chose to use the IUD.

Miller suggests that even though an individual's sexual and contraceptive behavior is determined by many different factors, it may
be possible to identify common themes as women move through
this three-step sequence and develop what he defined as "contraceptive vigilance." When trying to assess an individual's sexual and
contraceptive behavior, the present location of that woman in Miller's proposed developmental sequence must be identified. He infers
that with understanding of current usage and past behaviors, a care
provider may anticipate a woman's future behavior, which may
either enhance or detract from her contraceptive vigilance. The
concept of regression in this developmental sequence is addressed
only from the prospect that interactions with care providers work
either in the strengthening or the unlearning of contraceptive vigilance. He does not identify if the women's future goals and the care
providers' goals to maintain contraceptive vigilance by progressing
to the prescription methods were congruent.

In the 20 years since the data were collected for these two studies, additional methods of contraception have developed and society's attitude toward sexual activity and contraception have
changed. Using a phenomenological approach, Lethbridge (1991)
interviewed 30 women for the purpose of exploring women's experiences with contraception in general, their pathways through the
methods, and the nature of their decision making as they changed or
persisted with methods. Based on the theme of contraceptive vigilance, she reported the following categories: (1) choosing from
among limited options; (2) managing contraceptive use–short or
long term, consecutively or sequentially; (3) a fear of unwanted
pregnancy; (4) contraception as a woman's burden; (5) health care

system as contraceptive gatekeeper–both enabling and constraining; and (6) contraceptive accoutrement which describes the side effects and difficulties that accompany the use of various contraceptives.

SUMMARY

The purpose of this study was to generate data grounded in the experiences of fertility regulating women. The goal was to develop a substantive theory concerning the fertility regulating process of women and the factors that impact upon that process within their daily lives. A definitive need exists for the development of nursing knowledge based on the women's perspective when the care is related to women. This study is significant because it comprises the first step in developing interventions based on women's current needs concerning fertility regulation.

Even with the previous research, a complete understanding of the contraceptive adoption and retention patterns remains at a relatively rudimentary level. Systematic examination is needed of the method destinations of women who change methods, the reasons for these changes, and the factors that impact on these decisions. Such information is of direct relevance in understanding method prevalence, method differences in use-failure, and aggregate changes in the risks of unintended pregnancy. This study was designed to address this void, by using different processes to determine from women, across a broad spectrum of age, racial, social, and economic groups, the various factors that have influenced their past patterns of contraceptive use, and what strategies they anticipate using in the future. What developed is a fuller description of women's actual experiences with contraception within the conceptual and contextual frameworks of their lives.

REFERENCES

Bumpass, L. and Rindfuss, R. (1984). "The effect of marital dissolution on contraceptive practice." *Family Planning Perspectives* 16(6), pp. 271-274.

Forrest, J. D. (1987). "Unintended pregnancy among American Women," *Family Planning Perspectives,* 19(2), pp. 76-77.

Forrest, J. D. and Fordyce, R. P. (1988). "United States women's contraceptive attitudes and practice: How have they changed in the 1980s?" *Family Planning Perspectives,* 20(3), pp. 112-118.

Forrest, J. D. and Henshaw, S. K. (1983). "What U.S. women think and do about contraception." *Family Planning Perspectives,* 15(4), pp. 157-165.

Gerrard, M., McCann, L., and Geis, B. (1984). "The antecedents and prevention of unwanted pregnancy." In A. Rickle, M. Gerrard, and I. Iscoe (Eds.), *Social and psychological problems of women: Prevention and crises intervention* (pp. 85-101). New York: Hemisphere Publishing Co.

Grady, W. R., Hayward, M. D., and Florey, F. A. (1988). "Contraceptive discontinuation among married women in the United States." *Studies in Family Planning,* 19(4), pp. 227-235.

Grady, W. R., Hirsch, M. B., Keen, N., and Vaughan, B. (1983). "Contraceptive failure and continuation among married women in the United States, 1970-1975." *Studies in Family Planning,* 14(1), pp. 9-19.

Hammerslough, C. (1984). "Characteristics of women who stop using contraceptives." *Family Planning Perspectives,* 16(1), pp. 14-18.

Hatcher, R. A., Guest, R., Stewart, F., Stewart, G., Trussel, T., Cerel, S., and Cates, W. (1986). *Contraceptive Technology 1986-1987* (13th revised edition). New York: Irvington Publishing.

Krishnamoni, D. and Jain, S. (1985). "The use of contraception among abortion applicants." *Canadian Journal of Public Health,* 76(2), pp. 93-97.

Lethbridge, D. (1991). "Choosing and using contraception: Toward a theory of women's contraceptive self-care." *Nursing Research,* 40 (5), pp. 276-280.

Lindemann, C. (1972). *Birth control and unmarried women.* New York: Springer Publishing.

Miller, W. B. (1976). "Sexual and contraceptive behavior in young unmarried women." *Primary Care,* 3(3), pp. 427-453.

Mosher, W. and Pratt, W. (1990). "Contraceptive use in the United States, 1973-1988." *Advance Data from Vital and Health Statistics of the National Center for Health Statistics* (Number 182, March 20). Washington, DC: U.S. Department of Health and Human Services.

Ory, H., Forrest, J. D., and Lincoln, R. (1983). *Making choices: Evaluating health risks and benefits of birth control.* New York: Alan Guttmacher Institute.

Pratt, W. and Bachrach, C.A. (1987)."What do women use when they stop using the pill?" *Family Planning Perspectives,* 19(6), pp. 257-266.

Sawyer, R. and Beck, K. (1989). "Oral contraception: A survey of college women's concerns and experience." *Health Education,* 20(3), pp. 17-21.

Zelnick, M., Koenig, M., and Kim, Y. (1984). "Sources of prescription contraceptives and subsequent pregnancy among young women." *Family Planning Perspectives,* 16(1), pp. 6-13.

Appendix C
Research Design

THE PHENOMENA

The phenomena central to this study were the choices that women made while attempting to control their fertility. Any method or means that a woman considered to be beneficial to her in the prevention of pregnancy was included. The critical element was that the woman did not desire pregnancy. Women related their attempts to practice contraception within the contextual frameworks of their lives.

DESIGN OF THE STUDY

This study was designed to capture the lived experiences of women who are practicing contraception. Methods that take women's lived experience as the departure point for an investigation pay special attention to everyday complaints and treatments. Instead of taking the external observer perspective, these women's histories, comments, and complaints were explored with them in an attempt to understand their feelings about them (McBride and McBride, 1981).

Grounded theory provides a method for investigating previously unresearched areas and a new point of view in familiar situations (Stern, 1980). In this grounded theory study, the phenomena of women's fertility regulating patterns are discovered and explained within a theoretical framework that evolved during the research process itself. Conceptual categories, their conceptual properties, and generalized relationships among the categories and their properties, were developed by comparative analysis. Women shared many factors that they perceived to have determined their utilization of fertility regulation methods. Relevant categories and the relationships among them provided the basis from which the framework developed from the data (Strauss and Corbin, 1990).

Theoretical sensitivity, "the ability to recognize what is important in data and give it meaning" on the part of the researcher, was developed from previous reading, personal experience, and professional experiences with women attempting to control their fertility (Strauss and Corbin, 1990, p. 46). For this reason, the literature review was limited to the extent of determining if this phenomenon had been previously researched in this manner. Greater theoretical sensitivity developed as continual interaction with the data occurred.

Using a symbolic interactionist perspective, grounded theory provided a way to study how these women defined contraceptive events and how they acted in relation to these beliefs. Symbolic interactionism, as explained by Blumer (1969), involves three basic premises. First, "human beings act toward things on the basis of the meanings that the things have for them" (Blumer, 1969, p. 2). In this research, the human beings were women practicing contraception, and the event they were acting toward was the situation of intercourse with its risk of pregnancy.

The second premise is that "the meaning of such things is derived from, or arises out of the social interaction that one has with one's fellows" (Blumer, 1969, p. 2). The meaning of contraception, for a woman, grows out of the ways in which other people act toward her with regard to this activity. It is derived from the social interactions the woman may have with her partner, family, friends, health care providers, and/or others.

The third premise is that "meanings are handled in, and modified through an interpretive process used by the person in dealing with the things he encounters" (Blumer, 1969, p. 2). First, the woman indicates to herself the things toward which she is acting. Through this internalized communication, she identifies for herself the things that have meaning. Once identified, she interprets them in order to handle the meanings. The woman "selects, checks, suspends, regroups, and transforms the meanings in the light of the situation" in which she is placed (Blumer, 1969, p. 5). This interpretation becomes a formative process through which identified meanings are used as instruments for the guidance and formation of actions related to choice and use of fertility regulating methods. Therefore, to gain an understanding of the meaning of fertility regulating use patterns, each woman was interviewed concerning the influencing factors she could identify.

Triangulation, conceptualized as a type of multi-method approach, was used to attain completeness in revealing varied aspects of this phenomenon. Triangulation requires multiple sets of data, using different data sources and collection techniques, speaking to the same research question from different viewpoints (Brewer and Hunter, 1989; Knafl and Breitmayer, 1989). Each data source in this study contributed uniquely to the complete exploration. Unstructured interviews provided the opportunity for an in-depth investigation of the phenomenon, with both a historical and prospective focus, and the opportunity to explore from many aspects the variables these women viewed as affecting their method use during both unmarried and married states. Structured interviews, following a guide developed from previously collected data, provided an opportunity to explore in a more focused manner the historical data, current and future plans, and explanations of how and why variables affected their fertility control. Each collection method contributed a range of perceptions, some qualitatively described and others quantitatively represented.

By using both between-method and within-method triangulation, combining dissimilar sources and methods within the same analysis, a richer analysis was produced than could have been achieved by any method separately. This technique captures a more complete, holistic portrayal or thick description based predominantly on the qualitative data (Jick, 1983). Since different approaches to data collection produce different kinds of knowledge, combining them in this way will further enhance the possibility of discovering unique knowledge about women's use of fertility regulation methods (Hinds and Young, 1987).

Analysis of the three different data sets provided a descriptive account of the women's behaviors surrounding fertility regulation and their beliefs and concerns about the process of contraception. The qualitative and quantitative data were analyzed separately according to the principles of analysis germane to each type of data.

DATA GENERATION

Interviews

The data were generated through interviews and researcher field notes. Allport stated that ". . . if you wanted to know something about people's activities the best way of finding out was to ask them" (1942, p. 2). It is this willingness to treat the women as the heroines of their own drama, as valuable sources of particular information, that led to the choice of the interview for data collection in the next two segments. When the researcher and the respondent have the possibility of communicating directly with each other, the subtleties of the mutual understanding between the two parties can be established (Brenner, Brown, and Canter, 1985).

Unstructured Interviews

The exploratory approach of an unstructured interview fur-
nished a vehicle for interaction in the second segment of this
research. This technique provided the mechanism to uncover an
in-depth data base concerning the factors that have affected these
women's fertility regulation behaviors, as well as pertinent information concerning the respondents' receptivity to this line of
questioning and the frame of references that would lead to the
most generous responses. Based on the grounded theory methodology, data collection and analysis occurred simultaneously.

With the unstructured interviews, each woman was initially approached by telephone. After explaining the research project and its
purpose, she was asked to consider participating. Telephone contact
was chosen so that each subject might feel more able to refuse than
in a face-to-face contact. After each woman agreed to participate,
she then established the date, time, and location that would be
convenient to her for the interview. By allowing the women to
select the time and place, they could control the environment in
which they would disclose themselves. Three women chose to have
me come to their homes and two woman came to mine.

At the agreed-upon time, each interaction began with discussion on various other topics. As the participants' ease increased,
I then focused the discussion on the purpose of this contact. Each
woman was asked if the conversation could be recorded. Responses were in the affirmative, but were qualified with a facial
gesture or a verbal response of "if you really have to." None of
the conversations were taped because I interpreted the responses
to mean that the women were not completely comfortable with
the idea of audiotaping. They all agreed that notes could be taken
and that follow-up contact could occur for further data collection
and/or data verification.

The purpose of the research was again explained. Each participant was then asked to respond to, "Could you share with me

what fertility regulation has been like for you?" Each woman was encouraged to present her history in whatever manner she felt comfortable. All the women chose to present in chronological order (as different from method order, partner order, problem list, care provider, etc.).

During the unstructured interviews, each woman spoke on the topic in as much depth as she supposed was needed and as she desired. Dates and sequencing of specific events were elicited later in the interview so that the reporting of thoughts and feelings would not be interrupted and possibly lost in the attempt to get a date correct initially. Further questions, which developed during the interview, were tailored toward clarification or exploring further the unique experiences of each woman. The interviews continued with the respondents until no new data were forthcoming.

Some researchers express concern that respondents are not candid about personally sensitive information. Discussing the details of fertility regulation includes, to some extent, the discussion of a woman's sexual practices that are personal and may be very sensitive. However, in a Rand study, entitled "Response Errors in Sensitive Topic Surveys" it was determined that the average response bias for most sensitive topics is zero (Marquis et al., 1981). Their conclusions, based on many studies, did not support the hypothesis that people provide inaccurate information on topics that are sensitive, illegal, or viewed as socially unacceptable.

The necessary demographic information was obtained from the participants at the conclusion of the interview. To build trustworthiness, transcription of the notes was done immediately following the interview (Lincoln and Guba, 1985). If analysis revealed discrepancies or omissions in a data set, return interviews with the specific respondents were conducted. It was necessary to do return interviews in three cases, for clarification. As data from later respondents were analyzed and compared to items from previous respondents, earlier respondents were contacted and asked additional questions. This occurred with each of the four earlier participants.

Structured Interviews

The structured interviews were conducted in a private, non-profit women's health clinic. The clinic provided a small room adjacent to the clinic waiting room for privacy. Most prospective participants were approached at the clinic and asked if they would like to participate in a study concerning their use of contraception.

The initial interview guide, consisting of both open-ended and closed-ended questions, was developed based on factors revealed in the previous chart reviews and unstructured interviews. It was revised as new data were revealed, so these issues would be addressed with subsequent participants. The guidance provided by a structured interview format allowed for the collection of the greatest amount of data in the most efficient manner. To facilitate information gathering, method use patterns were requested in chronological order as favored by the participants in the unstructured interviews. Both open-ended and closed-ended questions were presented to the respondents allowing for further clarification of data, on particular items, if desired or necessary.

During the course of these interviews, if a respondent's answers were uncertain or unknown, the researcher returned to those items at the completion of the interview, with the understanding that recall of a respondent can be enhanced as the topic is covered in more detail. When conflicting data were obtained at different points in the interview, clarification was sought later in the interview, as ease with the interviewer and the topic increased. Demographic data were collected to describe this group of respondents. Accuracy of all data was protected by a preliminary transcribing of the interviewer's notes immediately following the session, rather than relying on the researcher's memory.

At the completion of each interview, the respondents were asked if they had any questions for me. About half of the women responded. Some wanted more information about future contraceptive options that might become available. Others were curious about how their personal experiences could help other women and wanted an explanation of how this research process could effect change. Some stated that having to think about their past behaviors and relationships opened up a new awareness for them. Many thanked me for being interested in their experiences, as no one else had ever seemed concerned. Valuing the women's efforts and expenditure of time, a statement to that effect and the presentation of $10 occurred after the interview. Five women refused to accept the money.

PROTECTION OF CONFIDENTIALITY

The protection of all participants' identities was considered at all times. Before the interviews, the research was fully explained and written consent was obtained. (Refer to Appendix B.) The participants understood that they might withdraw from participation at any time without fear of penalty. All data were identified by a code and keyed to a list of names kept in a separate location. All identification of the participants in any published findings is by code name or number only; when appropriate, data are reported only in the aggregate. No harmful procedures, situations, or materials that would be hazardous to the participants or the researcher occurred.

SAMPLE

To elicit the broadest amount of data, women were selected from two different sources for this investigation.

Unstructured Interviews

For the unstructured interviews, a group of women with an extended history of use of various methods of fertility regulation was needed to develop a pattern of fertility regulation across time. Using the constant comparative technique (Glaser and Strauss, 1967), a purposive convenience sample of women with diverse patterns of fertility regulation was selected sequentially. Each participant was approached based on known variations in her background. As each participant's responses were added to the data set, thought was then given to finding a respondent with an expected different life experience. The variable characteristics, based on questions raised from the chart reviews, were: (1) current age: 39.8 years; (2) education: completed high school–1, associate degree–1, BS–1, MS–2; (3) age at onset of sexual activity: 17 to 20 years of age, with a mean of 17.6; and (4) years of contraceptive activity: 19 to 26 years of age, with a mean of 22.2.

Structured Interviews

The structured interviews were conducted with clients seeking care from a free-standing, private, nonprofit women's health clinic. Twenty-five women who had made appointments for contraceptive care at the gynecological clinic were contacted to request their participation in the research interview. After the research was explained to them, they were asked to come to the clinic one hour before their scheduled appointment. Four of these women agreed to come. Two kept their appointments with me and two did not keep their clinic appointments. One of these women participated when she returned at a later date. The rest of the women refused when contacted, stating they did not anticipate having the time available.

The lack of efficiency of this method caused a reevaluation and subsequent change to the direct recruiting of participants. Women were approached either before or after they had received care at the clinic. The research was briefly explained to them. If they agreed, a written explanation of the research was provided for them to read, and consent forms were signed. Of the 54 women approached, 48 wished to participate, but only 31 had the time to do so. Two women asked to participate the next time they returned to the clinic and did so. A total of 35 women participated in the semistructured interviews. Age at interview ranged from 16 through 39, with a mean of 23.49 and a standard deviation of 5.29. The highest levels of education completed were: less than high school, 15.7 percent; high school, 21.9 percent; some college, 34.4 percent; BS or BA, 12.5 percent; and graduate school, 15.6 percent. Age at onset of sexual activity was: 15 to 16 years, 42.9 percent; 17 to 18 years, 25.7 percent; 19 to 20 years, 20.0 percent; 21 years and older, 11.5 percent, with a mean of 17.63 and standard deviation of 2.65.

All of the women were currently single, although two had been married previously. Twenty-five were in what they classified as a steady relationship, four were dating, and five were currently uninvolved in a dating relationship. Number of years of contraceptive experience ranged from less than one to more than 18 years with a mean of 5.91 and a standard deviation 4.61.

DATA ANALYSIS

Grounded theory, a qualitative methodology, was used to study the phenomenon of women's fertility regulation. Triangulation of data was accomplished by using different data sources and collection techniques. Data were collected through unstructured and structured interviews. The qualitative and quantitative data were analyzed separately according to the principles of analysis germane to each type of data. Trustworthiness (Lincoln and Guba, 1985) was facilitated by transcription of the notes immediately following the interview. Return interviews were held as needed.

The interviews were transcribed into a program developed as a research tool for handling qualitative data. Open coding of the interviews was accomplished by the investigator using this tool. Subsets of coded passages were then selected by code and exported to a word processing program. Coding and recoding of data allowed the categories and subcategories to become increasingly more apparent.

Properties and dimensions of each category were derived. "Properties are the characteristics or attributes of a category and . . . dimensions represent locations of a property along a continuum" (Strauss and Corbin, 1990, p. 69). For example, each woman reported her use of contraception and the sequence in which methods were used. These data were labeled "contraceptive method sequence" category. The properties, or characteristics of the methods, were labeled by differences in the process of procurement: prescription method (e.g., oral contraception) or nonprescription method (e.g., condom); by mechanism of action: barrier (e.g., diaphragm), systemic (e.g., oral contraception), chemical (e.g., spermicidal foam), or other (e.g., withdrawal); or by use: coital event specific (e.g., condoms) or nonevent specific (e.g., IUD). Within the category itself, each method had a known dimensional range–such as use-effectiveness, personal health risk, and method cost–which varied along a continuum. Since each category had several properties and each property varied over a dimensional continuum, each occurrence of a method sequence category could be given a separate dimensional profile. When these women's method profiles were grouped together, variations in patterns became evident (Strauss and Corbin, 1990).

Analysis of the data sets provided a descriptive account of the women's behaviors surrounding fertility regulation, and revealed the beliefs and concerns that they shared about the contraception process. Axial coding indicated that five major categories could be derived from the data. These categories are: (1) *Personalizing Pregnancy Risk*–the woman becomes aware that she can become pregnant and has options, (2) *Exploring Options*–an evaluation of preferences based on her conception of potential ramifications, followed by a response (3) *Using an Option*–the use of an intervention that the woman believes will reduce her chances of becoming pregnant, *(4) Contending with the Ramifications of Use*–identifies the actual consequences of her actions and evaluates the tradeoffs for her, and (5) *Contending with Use-Effectiveness Rates*–dealing with the monthly concern of unintended pregnancy.

While each woman's pattern of contraceptive use was unique, these categories represent the processes the women went through while attempting to manage their fertility. The categories are processual in nature and remain a part of a woman's life as long as she is concerned with controlling her fertility. The core category, *Advocating for Self,* evolved from these five categories.

REFERENCES

Allport, G.W. (1942). *The use of personal documents in psychological science.* New York: Social Sciences Research Council.

Blumer, H. (1969). *Symbolic interactionism: Perspective and method.* Englewood Cliffs, NJ: Prentice-Hall.

Brenner, M., Brown, J., and Canter, D. (1985). *The research interview: Uses and approaches.* Orlando, FL: Academic Press.

Brewer, J. and Hunter, A. (1989). *Multimethod research.* Newbury Park, CA: Sage.

Glaser, B. and Strauss, A. (1967). *The discovery of grounded theory-Strategies for qualitative research.* New York: Aldine De Gruyter.

Hinds, P.S. and Young, K.J. (1987). "A triangulation of methods and paradigms to study nurse-given wellness care." *Nursing Research,* 36(3), pp. 195-198.

Jick, T. (1983). "Mixing qualitative and quantitative methods: Triangulation in action." In J. Van Maanen (Ed.), *Qualitative methodology* (pp. 135-147). Beverly Hills, CA: Sage.

Knafl, K.A. and Breitmayer, B.J. (1989). "Triangulation in qualitative research: Issues of conceptual clarity and purpose." In J. M. Morse (Ed.), *Qualitative nursing research: A contemporary dialogue* (pp. 209-220) Rockville, MD: Aspen.

Lincoln, Y. and Guba, E. (1985). *Naturalistic inquiry.* Beverly Hills, CA: Sage.

Marquis, K., Duan, N., Marquis, M., and Polich, J. (1981). *Response errors in sensitive topic surveys.* R-2710/1-HHS. Santa Monica, CA: Rand.

McBride, A. and McBride, W. (1981). "Theoretical underpinnings for women's health." *Women and Health,* 6(1/2), pp. 37-55.

Stern, P. (1980). "Grounded theory methodology: Its uses and processes." *Image: Journal of Nursing Scholarship,* 12(1), pp. 20-23.

Strauss, A. and Corbin, J. (1990). *Basics of qualitative research-Grounded theory procedures and techniques.* Newbury Park, CA: Sage.

Appendix D
Portrait of the Women

Thirty women participated in the data collection interviews. They represent a cross-section of cultures, economic groups, and educational attainment. To provide the women with anonymity and yet give each participant full credit for her contribution, every woman is referred to by a code name.

UNSTRUCTURED INTERVIEW PARTICIPANTS

The five women of this data set are busy with home, work, and community obligations. Each of them is married and is raising children, ranging in age from 21 to 24. Each works at least 24 hours per week and three are working full-time outside the home. Each is involved with from one to four community activities. All verbalized that they volunteered their time for the interview due to an interest in helping other women. Their desire to help others and their trust of the researcher, based on past interactions, allowed them to be very open in their responses. They therefore provided information that they may not have offered to a stranger.

Each woman was selected sequentially for inclusion in this study based on known differences in life experiences. These women have a history of attempting to control their fertility for at least 19 years. They were born between 1945 and 1955 and became sexually active between 1965 and 1972, at the beginning of the relaxation of societal and legal restraints concerning access to birth control. They have maintained their sexual activity until the time of the study, creating a range of 19 to 26 years. Four women were sexually active before marriage. Three were raised in a Protestant denomination and two were raised in the Roman Catholic church.

All are white, were born and raised in the United States, and have spent most of their lives in eastern Massachusetts and Rhode Island. They are fairly well educated with: one high school diploma, one associate's degree, one bachelor's degree and two master's degrees. Financial status during the course of their fertility regulation has ranged from less than $10,000 as a single woman to over $50,000 as joint income with their partner. None of them has ever had health insurance that covered the cost of birth control methods. All visits for birth control care, except for the initial postpartum visits, were paid for out-of-pocket. The products they decided to use were seldom provided and had to be purchased.

Each woman has used from two to six different birth control methods. Collectively the five women have used 11 different methods for preventing unintended births. They reported having used the following methods singly or in tandem: withdrawal, rhythm, abstinence, condoms, foam and condoms, the diaphragm, an intrauterine device (IUD), oral contraception (the pill), sterilization, and therapeutic abortion.

STRUCTURED INTERVIEW PARTICIPANTS

The participants for this segment of the research were located through a private, nonprofit family planning clinic where these women had sought care. The women, constituting a convenience sample, were approached individually, and were interviewed over seven different days.

These 35 women were born during the years 1951 through 1974 and at the time of the study ranged in age from 16 to 39 (mean = 23.49, mode = 21, standard deviation = 5.294). As a group they are fairly well educated with 15.6 percent in or having completed graduate school, another 34.4 percent having had some college education, and 21.9 percent having completed high school. Currently 44.12 percent are full-time students at either the secondary, undergraduate, or the graduate level. When asked about access to money, 32.4 percent had less than $5,000, 29.4 percent less than $10,000, 8.8 percent less than $15,000, 11.8 percent less than $20,000, with the remaining six women reporting access to between $20,000 and $60,000. Although only 37.1 percent of the women were working full time, 68.6 percent had health insurance of some type. But only 26.5 percent had coverage that paid for birth control visits and products. The rest of the women paid for the visits and the method they chose out-of-pocket.

When asked to describe their current relationship 73.5 percent of the women labeled themselves as being in a steady relationship. The descriptions were of monogamous relationships, at least on the part of the woman, lasting over a period of time, and often with a shared domicile. Labeling their relationships as dating, 11.8 percent described new relationships or relationships without long-term commitment. Five of the women (14.7 percent) labeled themselves as currently uninvolved, due to a recent break-up of a relationship. Being "uninvolved" could not be interpreted as not being sexually active. Several respondents had been married previously but were no longer in these relationships.

These women have individual histories of attempting to practice contraception for zero to 18 years (mean = 5.9, standard deviation = 4.617) and a combined history of 207 years. When asked the ways she knew to prevent pregnancy, each woman recalled at least two ways. Some women stated as many as 13 ways, however the mean number was 6.06 with a standard deviation of 2.9. With the extent of knowledge these women possessed, they used from one to seven methods (mean = 3.2, standard deviation = 1.65, mode = 3). They changed between the methods they used from one to 12 times (mean = 4.23, standard deviation = 2.87, mode = 3). In their individual processes of using contraceptives they, as a group, changed methods a total of 148 times.

During their 207 years of practicing contraception, 22 women experienced a total of 40 pregnancies. Forty percent of these women had two pregnancies and 37.1 percent had one pregnancy. Of these 40 pregnancies, five were desired at the time they occurred. The rest were unplanned and undesired at the time of conception and occurred due to method failure, use failure, or lack of contraceptive precaution. The outcomes of these pregnancies were 30 therapeutic abortions, nine births, and one spontaneous abortion.

The information provided by these 40 women was personal, individually unique, and diverse in nature. However, when their method use profiles were developed into categories, commonalities became evident. This research approach allowed the women to share in the analysis of the conditions of their lives and gathered data that will improve understanding of these women's fertility regulating concerns.

Appendix E
Assessment Guide to Assist in Success

The following are questions to be explored with a woman initiating a new contraceptive choice. These areas of concern may be explored in any order; however, each area of concern must be addressed.

Availability

Where will you obtain (method) from?
Where will you store it (them) for easy access? for confidentiality?
Will this be convenient so it (they) will be available when you need it (them)?
With the pill–When during the day will you take it? How will you deal with variable times such as on the weekend? What will you use with the pill when you need to take antibiotics?

Cost

Do you know how much (method) cost? At what point would cost become a problem?
What other methods do you have available?

Use-Comfort Level

Do you have any concerns about possible side effects from (method)? What effects do you expect?
How will using the (method) affect your sexual pleasure? Your

partner's sexual pleasure? What will you do if this is uncomfortable when you use it?

Support System

Have any of your family or friends used (method)? What did they say about it? Will you tell them you're using it?
Do your religious beliefs support the use of (method)?
How does that make you feel?
How does your partner feel about (method)?

Level of Conviction

What would happen in your life if you become pregnant?
What would cause you to use a back-up system?
What will it be? Where will you get it?
Do you anticipate any problems starting (method)?
Is there any way that I may help so that it (the process of contraception) is easier for you?

Index

Abandonment, fear of, 90
Abstinence, 3,20
Advocating for Self, 9-14,87-96
  exploring options, 11-12
  model, 11,14
  origin of categories in, 121-122
  personalizing pregnancy risk,
    10-11,13-14
  ramifications of use, 13-14
  theory of, 87-89
  using options, 12
Advocating for Self study
  data analysis in, 120-122
  data, generation of, 114-118
  demographics of, 119-120,
    125-128
  design of, 111-114
  genesis of, 101-109
  goal of, 109
  interviews in, 114-120
  literature review for, 102-106
  protection of confidentiality
    in, 118
Allport, G. W., 114
Analysis of data, 120-122
Assessment guide, 129-130
Assumptions about women's
    contraception, 3-8
  and acceptance of sexuality, 5
  lack of access to, 5
  conflict about methods of, 6
  fears of, 5-6
  ignorance of methods of, 4
  patterns of use of, 7-8
  and unprotected intercourse, 6
Audiotaping, 115
Availability of contraceptives, 129

Barrier methods
  reactions to use of, 53-55
Beliefs. *See* Assumptions
Bladder infections, 61-62
Bumpass, L., 103

Cervical cap, 53-54,66
Changes in body. *See* Physical
    ramifications of
    contraception
Choice, patterns of, 75-86
Client, 99
Condoms, 3
  effects of, 60,61
  reactions to use of, 54-55,64
  use of, 48-49,66
Confidentiality, 118
Contraception
  after pregnancy, 70-71
  awareness of options and use, 20
  benefits of, 1-2
  and changes in relationships,
    25-26
  decision process for, 10-14,95
  expense of, 22
  exploring options for, 11-12,29-43
  factors in choosing method
    of, 95-96
  fears of, 5-6
  influence of others on,
    23-25,39-42
  influence of partners on, 20-23,
    38-39,49-52,89-90
  in marriage, 22-23
  ramifications of, 59-73
  studies of, 102-109